HOW DO I GET THEM TO WRITE?

Explore the reading-writing connection using freewriting and mentor texts to motivate and empower students

Karen Filewych

Pembroke Publishers Limited

To Mom and Dad:
For inspiring my love of language

© **2017 Pembroke Publishers**
538 Hood Road
Markham, Ontario, Canada L3R 3K9
www.pembrokepublishers.com

Distributed in the U.S. by Stenhouse Publishers
PO Box 11020
Portland, ME 04104-7020
www.stenhouse.com

Library and Archives Canada Cataloguing in Publication

Filewych, Karen, author

   How do I get them to write? : explore the reading-writing connection using freewriting and mentor texts to motivate and empower students / Karen Filewych.

Issued in print and electronic formats.
ISBN 978-1-55138-322-4 (softcover).--ISBN 978-1-55138-923-3 (PDF)

   1. English language--Writing--Study and teaching (Elementary). 2. Language arts (Elementary). I. Title.

LB1576.F43 2017   372.62'3044   C2017-901910-4
                                     C2017-901911-2

Editor: Kate Revington
Cover Design: John Zehethofer
Typesetting: Jay Tee Graphics Ltd.

Printed and bound in Canada
9 8 7 6 5 4 3 2 1

Contents

Acknowledgments

This book has been a labor of love years in the making. It would not be in your hands without the assistance and support of many people.

Thanks and appreciation go

- to my students, who bring delight and joy to each day of work
- to my colleagues at St. Charles School, for putting up with me and my ideas
- to my admin partners, Dan and Tisa, for your support of my "writing days" and faith in my projects

Thanks also go

- to Alessandra, Donatella, Aubrey, Marcus, Drew, Ava, Penny, Will, Sydney, and Harper for your exciting contributions
- to the readers of my drafts, for your time and insight: Christina, Sam, Nicole, Rose, Laurie, Cheryl, Katrina, Lisa, Laura, and especially Mom, who has read many versions of this text
- to the Pembroke team: Mary, for your belief in my book from the beginning, and Kate, for your expertise and attention to detail

Finally, I give thanks

- to my family, for fully supporting my passion and enduring my eccentricities
- and, most important, to Dan, for your patience and ear as I rambled on about my manuscript. Your love and support mean the world to me.

Introduction: To Write and to Teach

I love to write. I write for many reasons. I write to reflect and to inspire. I write to release my creativity. I write to learn about the world around me. I write because I feel the need to write. Few things satisfy me more than the time I spend writing.

I also love to teach. There is such promise in the youth before us. Watching a student grasp a difficult concept, hearing a student new to Canada and our language speak in front of the class for the first time, or witnessing the moment when this skill called reading becomes real for a child — this is why I teach. I want to help my students fulfill their promise.

So, when I have the opportunity to teach writing to my students, well, my two passions fuel each other.

I know that many others find it daunting to teach writing to their students, however. Just as I feel intimidated by the thought of teaching science and sometimes even math, I understand that many teachers feel this way about writing. So, this book is meant as a tool for teaching writing. Whether you enjoy writing or are intimidated by it, this will be a valuable reference in creating a productive writing environment for your students.

Writing as a Cross-Curricular Skill

When I consider writing in the classroom setting, I see two main functions: *learning to write* (something we know is in the curriculum and must teach) and *writing to learn* (a less talked-about function of writing in the classroom). I have not divided the book into sections to delineate these two functions. Ideally, in the classroom these functions dance and mingle throughout the day.

Although writing is a skill covered in our language arts curriculum, I am going to challenge you to think about how writing can fit into all areas of the curriculum. Students can — and should — write within every subject. In this way, they will be *writing to learn*.

While this book is primarily about writing, you are going to discover the many ways in which I use *reading* to teach writing. The connection between the two cannot be downplayed: they go hand in hand. Reading and writing help our students engage more fully in all aspects of the lives they live. Through reading, writing, and the inevitable discussions that follow, our students can learn from the experiences of others, open their minds to many possibilities, gain a glimpse of worlds unknown to them, make connections to their own lives, reflect on their own choices, and contextualize their learning. When we provide students with this time to read and explore texts — texts that may reflect their lives or open doors to other worlds — and then to write about what they think, what they feel, and how they connect to the texts read, the experience is powerful. Adrienne Gear (2011) suggests,

> Writing to engage thinking can, in fact, help change our focus and purpose for writing in school, and can perhaps help students develop a greater sense of the reader–writer connection. (p. 12)

Students begin to see writing as something more than an assignment to be handed in to their teacher. They begin to understand how reading and writing, and the interplay between the two, can lead to deeper thinking.

Our curricular focus has shifted from separate, isolated subjects that fit into precise blocks of time; we are now encouraged to integrate and teach skills that carry students across the curriculum. If we want our writing experiences to be authentic, writing cannot occur only in language arts. We must cross disciplinary boundaries. As Marion Crowhurst (1993) says,

> … the emphasis in the classroom should be on using language to do real things, rather than on dummy-run exercises for practice. In this way, children will use authentic language for real purposes. They will read real texts to find out or to enjoy. They won't read texts to practice reading skills. They will write for authentic purposes — to entertain, inform, invite, thank, or persuade the teacher, the principal, their peers or the readers of the community newspaper. (p. 8)

Effective teachers have come to understand how to integrate their subjects, how to utilize their time wisely by having students read and write across the curriculum. *Writing to learn* is not a new concept. It is, however, being integrated into the classroom on a much more regular basis and certainly more successfully. Traditionally, most teachers were taught to think of writing strictly as a final product; however, writing is a process that can help students discover, create, and think critically in all disciplines of study. Through their writing experiences, students will construct meaning across the curriculum.

Writing as an Essential Life Skill

Writing is also a skill that students will carry with them beyond the four walls of our classrooms. The *Ontario Language Curriculum* expresses the idea in this way: "Learning to communicate with clarity and precision, orally, in writing, and through a variety of media, will help students to thrive in the world beyond school" (2006, 4). As important as it is for students to view writing as functional for school, we also want them to understand the power it can hold in their lives. The written word serves practical, utilitarian functions such as street signs, labels, and store names. It also serves more lofty purposes: expressing one's ideas and ideals, giving permanence to one's thoughts, advocating for the greater good, and exploring metaphysical ideas.

Our goal, then, is to give our students an environment where they feel comfortable putting pencil to paper or fingers to keyboard, taking the necessary risks involved in the writing process.

Writing as a Craft That Can Be Taught

I want more than that, though. Not only do I want my students to write — I want them to *enjoy* writing! I want them to view writing not as a distasteful chore, but as an exciting adventure.

But how best to achieve this ... The two most common mistakes I see teachers make when teaching writing is that their students do not write enough or there is little deliberate instruction about writing. Both are critical to our students' success. As I say to my students, simply talking about basketball will not help us to become better basketball players: we must also practise. The same is true for writing. Ideally, our students will be writing *something* daily. Fear not! With appropriate planning, this goal is quite easily accomplished. And there is certainly no need to assess everything our students write. I know that teachers work exceptionally hard and the demands sometimes seem endless. The role of this text is to make the teaching of curriculum more manageable.

The good news? Writing is a craft and can, therefore, be taught. Yes, it's true that some individuals are gifted with natural talent in this area; however, all can learn to write more effectively with appropriate teaching, modelling, and practice. Lucy Calkins speaks to the important role of the teacher:

> Children deserve to be explicitly taught the skills and strategies of effective writing, and the qualities of good writing. This teaching will be dramatically more powerful if teachers are studying the teaching of writing and if they are responsive to what students are doing and trying to do as writers. Children also deserve a teacher who demonstrates a commitment to writing. (2006, 10)

Our students must spend time engaged in the process of writing *and* be taught how to improve their writing: both are necessary.

Teaching Writing: A Gift of Empowerment

At the beginning of my career, I taught Grade 1. I saw how language, specifically learning to read and write, could empower students. It was thrilling to see student confidence levels flourish as they discovered the significance of a letter, a word, a sentence, a story. I was energized by the look of surprise on the students' faces when they became impressed with their own reading or writing. I also noticed the frustration of those who did not easily learn the skills involved in literacy.

I loved teaching Grade 1. In fact, I thought I'd teach Grade 1 forever. The progress the students made during the year was incredibly obvious, immediate, and exhilarating. The students revelled in the excitement of reading on their own for the first time or discovering new words.

Yet, as I began teaching older students (somewhat reluctantly I might add), I soon realized that the progress these students made was just as thrilling ... though perhaps not as obvious or immediate as it was in Grade 1. I realized that these students, too, need excellent instruction in language arts; they may not be *beginning* readers and writers, but effective and purposeful instruction can empower students of all ages to become more competent, confident individuals. In retrospect, I am grateful that I was open to a change in grade level: ultimately, it changed my thought process.

The ideas within this book stem from my experiences teaching students from Kindergarten to Grade 6. They have also been inspired by the many excellent teachers I have encountered over the years. No less, however, they have been influenced by experts such as Peter Elbow, Mem Fox, Nancie Atwell, Regie Routman, Lucy Calkins, Natalie Goldberg, Donald H. Graves, Tony Stead, Donald M. Murray, Adrienne Gear, and many language learning theorists.

Teaching students the skill of writing is a gift of empowerment: words change worlds.

1

Developing a Community of Learners

"For a community to be whole and healthy, it must be based on people's love and concern for each other."
— Millard Fuller

What is a chapter on creating a community of learners doing in a book about writing? I believe that one of the critical elements of the teaching of writing is the climate within the classroom. After all, writing makes us vulnerable. Before you can stimulate effective writing and effective dialogue about the writing, you must establish a community of learners.

Have you ever experienced the buzz of creative or intellectual energy? As a student? As a teacher? This energy originates in provocative and motivating environments. There are times when these situations *just happen*; more often though, this energy is created when someone establishes a community of learners where individuals feel safe, inspired, and engaged. As a teacher, I strive to create this environment with my students; as an administrator, I strive to create this atmosphere with my staff.

Ongoing Modelling and Dialogue

The most memorable moments of my career occurred when students provided each other with support, acceptance, and motivation. I do not believe that this comes naturally for all students: it is something we have to teach, model, and reinforce within our classrooms. When we teach our students that we all have strengths and areas in which we feel vulnerable, they learn to respect their peers despite their differences. Whether a student has pimples or glasses, diabetes or autism, students all deserve to be respected and valued simply because they are human. Ensuring that they realize this is not accomplished through a one-time-only discussion but by ongoing modelling and dialogue. In my classroom, I teach my students that each of us, myself included, strives towards our personal best. That personal best will look different for each individual, and there is no room or need for comparison. My classroom is not the place for competition but for cooperation: we support each other as we strive to reach our goals.

Our classroom environments and our schools should be places where our students feel safe enough to take risks. The underlying expectation in my class is always one of mutual respect. It is essential that we model appropriate word choice and tone to develop the environment we expect. We must be explicit in our expectations, acknowledging appropriate responses and discouraging inappropriate ones. Even subtleties such as body language and eye contact should be discussed with students. Students need to understand that their silent vocabulary — their posture, a raised eyebrow, how they sit, if they make or avoid eye contact — all communicate to those around them, sometimes unintentionally. Ultimately, our students will be grateful that they are in an environment where they feel respected, safe, and secure.

Consider for a moment something that does not come naturally to you, something you consider difficult. Now imagine that you have to perform this task or activity in front of a group of your peers day after day. What are the feelings evoked — anxiety, fear, inadequacy, embarrassment? This is likely how our students feel when we ask them to do something they find challenging, especially in front of their classmates. Once they have come to appreciate the varying ability levels — the strengths and challenges — within the classroom, though, students will be more willing to take risks.

A Transformative Moment: "I Need ..."

I remember a student who had not "fit in" during his entire academic career; it seemed he had learned, consciously and likely somewhat unconsciously, to invite the taunting and criticism he was subject to. The first day of Grade 6, I watched as he ran outside at recess, flailing his arms and repeatedly announcing, "I am cra-zee!" Being an outcast and a victim became his identity. He was an easy target with low self-esteem. Each day, I spoke to John* as I would to other students, showing that I valued him as a person, trying to include him in our community of learners.

In class, John's writing was filled with hostility and violence, mayhem and blood. Ironically, at the time he was in my class I was in a postgraduate university course where we were exploring ideas of censorship. I did not censor his writing or give him the reaction he expected. Instead, I responded positively to anything I could find positive to respond to. Despite my efforts, he seemed determined to act out and live up to the role of outcast that had been defined for him or perhaps that he had defined for himself.

And then one day we had a moment in class, stemming from a freewrite, which changed the dynamics of the classroom for the remainder of the year. Our writing prompt was "I need ..." As was typical, after rereading our own entries quietly to ourselves, I gave the students the opportunity to share their writing with the class. Several students read, I read, each of us with a different focus: some on basic needs, some on family, some stream-of-consciousness writing jumping from thought to thought. We enjoyed hearing how the same prompt had led us to write about an array of topics, and many of us were surprised at where our thoughts took us through our writing. We were engaged in a truly literary conversation.

Risky Writing in a Safe Place

Just as we were about to move on with the lesson, John asked to read his writing out loud. The students sat in silence as his words leapt from his page and resonated within our classroom. "I need to feel wanted. I need a friend." The silence

*Pseudonym used to protect the identity of the student.

deepened, and I noticed some nervous, awkward glances around the classroom. Though the words were simple, his topic was much more personal, poignant, and more immediately significant than the others had been, including my own. He was tentative at first and then with more conviction, he shared his feelings of isolation and despair.

As I listened, I felt the tears welling up and as I looked around the class, I knew I was not alone. "I wish I could just be normal and not afraid to come to school." His words continued to resonate within the classroom and when he finished, the students began to clap. Tears filled John's eyes. The change in the air was palpable.

The recess bell rang, releasing us from this defining moment. As the students stood to leave the room, they passed by John's desk where he still sat, almost motionless. Students who had never spoken to him before (and students who had only taunted or teased him before) shared their compliments and apologies. His entire demeanor changed that day: he began to walk differently and talk differently. Over time, he began interacting with his peers in more appropriate ways.

When John was reading aloud to the class, I felt as though I could sweep the air with my hand and feel the empathy, the regret, and the compassion in the room. His voice had transcended his usual writing abilities. He was not typically an especially strong writer as compared to many of his peers. Yet *this* writing was different. And why? I believe it was because he had something to say. He described his reluctance to attend school for fear of what the day would bring. He articulated years of anguish and resentment, longing and hurt. Though his words were simple, the meaning was profound.

On that fateful October day, written language connected us in unexpected ways. Through this piece of writing, the other students, for the first time, saw John as human and vulnerable. His writing revealed details and information about his life that created a sense of empathy.

Would John ever have shared these details if not through the process of writing? I don't believe so. Would he ever have shared his writing if he didn't feel he was in a safe environment? Again, I don't believe so. Those moments that surrounded a simple freewrite helped John to move beyond the constraints he had placed on himself, improved the overall dynamics of our classroom, and significantly influenced my career. Those moments also reinforced my instincts about the power of words.

What Our Classroom Environment Must Be

My goal as a teacher is to inspire my students to be caring and contributing members of society, and one way to further this is in the classroom, a social environment, a microcosm of the larger society. It is essential that we build trust within our classrooms to permit students to experiment with their identities and roles as members of society. Our environment must be safe enough to allow our students to take risks and not feel the pressure to give predetermined "right" answers. Our environment must be safe enough to encourage our students to think outside the proverbial box, to try on various perspectives and personas, and to test the status quo. Our environment must be safe enough to provide children like John with an opportunity to explore their anger and confusion and, it is hoped, arrive at a new awareness of self. My hope is that John found a bit of normalcy and acceptance within our classroom and that he was able to carry those feelings forward as he moved beyond our classroom environment. This moment with John emerged in a safe, productive environment: an environment rooted in love and respect. Though we can't create the moments, we can work to create the environment.

The Power of Words

Within our role as educators comes the responsibility to teach our students the power of words. As children, most of us enter into the world of language excited at our newfound means of communication. And yet, at times we are unprepared for the power of words. The combinations of letters, which form words, which then create phrases and sentences, have the power to hurt as well as help. The familiar chant, "sticks and stones may break my bones, but words will never hurt me" rings untrue for anyone who has experienced the painful sting of callous words. Words can be excruciatingly painful. The torment experienced by those bullied, not with fists but by language, must not be underestimated. Words spoken in mere seconds or etched on a bathroom wall can affect a person's life indefinitely.

A more recent phenomenon is the act of cyber bullying. The Internet gives bullies the illusion of anonymity and a wider audience for their cruel and insensitive words. Unfortunately, the news has been riddled with these incidents as of late and lawmakers struggle with how to define *cyber bullying* and prosecute the perpetrators. In the meantime, victims live with unrelenting torment. An onerous responsibility, then, is to create an environment where students understand the dichotomy and the delicate balance between freedom of speech and the potential of words to cause anguish. Though we cannot control what our students do or say, we can help them understand the power of words and nurture a compassion for others.

An Illustration

Use a tube of toothpaste to illustrate the power of words. Put students into small groups and give each group a tube of toothpaste. Tell them the toothpaste represents words. Challenge the students to discover the analogy on their own before demonstrating it to them. The lesson: Just as the toothpaste squeezed out of the tube cannot be put back inside, once words are out of our mouths, they cannot be taken back. Words can sometimes create a mess difficult or even impossible to clean up. Used correctly and responsibly, words can be helpful and bring joy, just as toothpaste used correctly and responsibly cleans our teeth and keeps us healthy. Students will remember this kinesthetic and visual experience.

The Language You Use as Teacher

Get into the habit of referring to your students as *readers* and *writers*. For example: "Okay, readers. What do you notice about the author's word choice on this page?" "Writers, pencils down. Take a few quiet moments to read what you've written today." It may seem a simple point, but by using this vocabulary with your students, it becomes a self-fulfilling prophecy. You set the expectation that they will succeed as readers and writers, indeed, that they *are* readers and writers. Students begin to see themselves as such and the tasks of reading and writing lose the feeling of something they are doing for school and, instead, become more authentic. They aren't *learning to become* readers and writers: they *are* readers and writers.

Be conscious, too, of the general language you use with your students: the tone, word choice, and intonation. Be wary of sarcasm and condescension. Your students look to you for guidance. Treat all students in your class with the same level of respect, and students will tend to do the same with their peers. If this is established in a general sense, it carries over into everything you do, including writing and peer feedback.

Your Influence as Teacher

Making strong connections with our students is the foundation of their learning: we cannot underestimate its power. I have witnessed students give up in despair because their teachers did not display confidence in them. On the other hand, I have witnessed students who have worked beyond their presumed potential because their teachers believed in them. Our students should trust us and see us as significant adults in their lives. This is especially true in elementary school where we see our students for prolonged periods. Many parents now work multiple jobs and there seems to be a tendency to over-schedule children in activities, sometimes limiting a child's meaningful contact with parents or guardians. For many students, the most significant, sustained contact is with you, the teacher.

Therefore, when planning our lessons and our year, it is essential that we consider how we can connect to our students not only on a cognitive level, but on an emotional level.

> We need to ask whether education for literacy can occur solely through the mind. We need to wonder about the role of the *affective* as well as the cognitive, in learning to read or write anything. Are the bones and the marrow being left on the shelf? (Fox 1993, 117)

Although classrooms are not bedrooms with cozy quilts and nightly bedtime stories, they can be safe spaces in which to engage in literacy pursuits. Providing students with a positive, nurturing, and constructive environment will directly influence their view of learning and further enable them to function in a highly literate world.

Should we expect a child who has never had intimate and cherished relations with the written word to pick up a book, or a pen, with the same enthusiasm as those of us who have deep emotional associations with books? Furthermore, consider those children whose only emotional connections to books are ones of frustration and exclusion as the words on the page are inaccessible to them. If a child has not had positive experiences with literature or language, then I as the teacher must be sure to show my enthusiasm and passion for the words on a page. The task is not difficult for a lover of language like myself, but it is one that cannot be ignored in an education world fraught with standardized testing, accountability, and assessment.

An Inviting Physical Environment

A well-planned physical environment can also contribute to creating a productive and inspiring space for your community of learners. The physical environment in your classroom should reflect the overall tone you wish to create. Does your classroom invite literacy, collaboration, and innovation? Does it have comfortable reading and writing spaces? Is it chaotic and cluttered or calming and organized? teacher centred or child centred? stifling or stimulating?

Have you noticed that students tend to mimic the habits of their teachers? A messy teacher often has a classroom full of messy students. Highly organized teachers tend to foster organizational skills and habits in their students.

Even if you are not changing classrooms, take the time to de-clutter and re-examine your own classroom environment. Sometimes it takes an outside perspective for us to see our own environments objectively; consider inviting a teacher you trust into your class for another opinion. Look at your environment from a child's point of view, too. The strategic arrangement of furniture and a healthy collection of literature, easily accessible to our students, can help promote an environment of learning.

A Fresh Start

Not long ago we asked our teachers to move classrooms because we wanted to reorganize our overall school layout. In addition to the expected benefits, there were some added rewards. Most teachers culled their classrooms significantly as they packed up and moved from one space to the other. As teachers set up their new classrooms, they re-examined the environment they wanted to create: everything from color scheme to layout. As I walked from room to room in the fall after the move, I noticed that teachers deliberately created nooks and crannies, and a variety of seating options. I also noticed less cluttered, more organized, and much calmer environments. In our classrooms, less is more.

An Inspiration Station

Create an Inspiration Station in your classroom for students to access. Include a variety of pens, pencils, paper, stationery, Post-it notes, and envelopes. Provide interesting objects and change them periodically. The possibilities are endless and students are thrilled when they discover new items or materials at the station.

After you introduce the Inspiration Station to your students, work together to generate a list of as many forms of writing as they can think of: stories, signs, shopping lists, letters, instructions, game rules, reports, recipes, book reviews, biographies, brochures, poems, posters, and so on. Keep this list at the Inspiration Station so students can refer to it when looking for something to write. This station is always popular during free time and for fast finishers, but it also provides inspiration during our regular writing time. (More information specific to narrative writing will be provided in Chapter 6.)

Positive Graffiti

Dynamic Documentation

One June day, as we were cleaning up the class, spontaneously, students began tearing away pieces of our graffiti wall to take away as souvenirs. The graffiti wall had become a fascinating, dynamic documentation of our year as a class: a way of giving ourselves a voice as individuals and as a collective.

To further develop your community of learners and to foster an encouraging environment, create a positive graffiti wall in the classroom. I use brown packing paper to cover a small bulletin board. I draw a few bricks here and there to make it look like an outside wall. On the first day of school each of us writes our names on the wall. During the remainder of the year, the students add to the board at their leisure with the only stipulation being that whatever they add — quotations, photographs, drawings, cartoons, words — must be positive. (Note: Have students use tape, not staples.) I also warn the students that their words or pictures might eventually be covered up as we overlap and add items.

Morning Meetings: A Positive Peer Dynamic

To help develop a community of learners, establish the practice of regular morning meetings. By coming together each morning, greeting each other, talking about the upcoming day, even praying together if you are in a faith-based school, you are building community within your classroom. These meetings can also empower students to deal with concerns and solve problems that might arise with their peers. Students begin to understand how they are responsible for their own behavior and how their behavior affects others.

Use this Henry Ford quotation to initiate discussion with students: "Coming together is a beginning, keeping together is progress, and working together is success."

Initially, you may find that a handful of students dominate your morning meetings. Work to ensure that all students feel comfortable contributing during the morning meeting but then also during all situations throughout the day. As Regie Routman (2014, 54) suggests, "One of our goals as educators must be to create learning environments that encourage student talk and honor students' thinking." During a morning meeting, you as the teacher are present to ensure that students interact with both kindness and respect. At other times, students will meet regularly in smaller collaborative groups, and you will not be present during all of their interactions. Consistent morning meetings help to maintain a positive peer dynamic in your learning environment which extends to all collaborative situations, including writing groups.

Writing Groups: Learning to Work in Harmony

To further develop a community of learners, it is essential to teach students what is expected when they work together in small groups. When we ask our students to collaborate, we sometimes assume that they know the expectations in a small-group setting. And yet, depending on their background or prior experience, they may not have the skills required to collaborate effectively. An analogy accessible to most students is that of an orchestra: the variety of instruments come together to create harmonious music. Without each member of the orchestra learning both the instrument and the musical score, the result is simply an awful lot of noise. Yet, each member of the orchestra, just like each member of the group, has a distinct role and contribution. Before working in a group, students should know how to give and receive feedback, contribute to the group without dominating, share the workload, utilize the strengths of each group member, and share the credit of a job well done. We must teach our students the specific language and skills expected during collaboration so they can contribute harmoniously.

One of the strategies I find most effective in further improving student writing is to implement writing groups: groups of three or four students who share their writing and give and receive feedback. To ensure a balance of personalities and ability levels, I compose the groups myself. To ensure a comfort level for my students, I let them choose their own pieces of writing: they are then excited and proud to share rather than reluctant. Before the students first go into their groups, I spend time modelling responses and discussing the difference between criticism and constructive criticism. I give outrageous examples of criticism so they begin to understand what is appropriate and what is not. We discuss comments like "That sucks!" or "That's silly." I encourage students to consider how they would feel as a writer if they were to hear such comments.

After this initial discussion, I then offer more subtle examples. I might, for example, ask the students which statement they would rather hear: "that doesn't make any sense" or "your idea is interesting, but I'm not sure I understand this part here." The students can compare the comments and begin to understand how the first comment could defeat a writer and how the second comment could support the writer in improving the work. We talk about body language and tone of voice to ensure that we continue to respect each member of our community of learners.

From Oral Prompts to Written Feedback

You can adjust the prompt pages depending on the grade level you teach, or you might limit the number of prompts if there is specific feedback you want your students to focus on for a particular day.

The structure of the first writing group meetings is quite formalized, with prompts the students can use to respond to their peers. I give the students a small page to refer to. Initially, students respond to their peers orally, prompts in hand as a reminder. Below is a form featuring the sorts of prompts I provide.

Writing Group Prompts

My favorite part of your writing is …
I like the way you …
Could you explain …
Have you considered …
I'd like to hear more about …
In class we've been discussing _____. I noticed that you …

Remember, stay positive and respect your peers!

As they become more comfortable in their groups, responses become more natural and most students no longer rely on the prompts. In the larger context of our community of learners, the students build trust within their smaller community of writers.

Eventually, I have students provide written responses to their peers on feedback strips (examples provided in Chapters 4, 6, and 7) in addition to taking part in discussion. After the writing group session, these feedback strips are given to the writers, and they staple them to their work to refer to during editing and revising. These feedback strips accomplish two things: first, they guide the listeners as to what kind of feedback to give, and second, they provide the writers with suggestions they can refer to as they continue working on their writing.

The time within writing groups is time well spent. The students learn to give and receive feedback, appreciate the responses of their peers, and ultimately become excited to return to their desks and revise their work. Generally, I keep the writing groups the same throughout the year with minor changes as necessary. The communication skills students learn in writing groups transfer to many aspects of their lives.

Gallery Walks: "I Like …"

Depending on what students are viewing, they may not have time to see the work of all of their peers.

During a gallery walk, students explore the work of their peers. This process works best for visual journal entries, poetry, and reader response journals. Obviously, a respectful, positive classroom atmosphere is necessary for this process to work. Students put their own work on their desks and then walk around, quietly viewing and reading the work of their peers.

Students can be given specific instructions during the gallery walk or it could simply be an opportunity to see what others have done. Sometimes, I give students Post-it notes and ask them to write an *I like* statement for two of their peers. Students know that every student should have two *I like* statements on his or her desk by the end of the gallery walk.

It is also effective to have a class discussion after a gallery walk. Simply ask the question, "What did you notice?" Students respectfully share what they noticed; there is no need to mention their classmates by name.

Moving Forward

The four walls of a classroom do not necessarily translate into a community of learners — this community must be created. If we walk into our classrooms and assume that our students know what is expected, know what we value, and know how to behave, we set ourselves and our students up for failure. On the other hand, if we value student differences and student engagement, if we teach our students the behavior we expect, our students will respond with attention, inquisitiveness, and optimism. By establishing a community of learners, we set the foundation for the teaching of reading, writing, thinking, and creating.

But with a community of learners, we can achieve more. My desire is that students leave my classroom knowing how it feels to be valued and appreciated for who they are, with the confidence to stand up for what is right and the dignity to respect differences in our world. My desire, too, is that they leave my classroom with hope in our world and faith in themselves. Whether or not you have articulated this, you likely desire the same for your students. The creation of communities of learners in our classrooms and schools promotes this long-term goal.

2

Setting Up the Year: Planning and Preparation

"Always, always have a plan."
— Rick Riordan

When I began writing this book, I dialogued with many teachers to determine what they wanted from a book about the teaching of writing. Overwhelmingly, they asked for a chapter on organizing and planning their language arts curriculum. This chapter attempts to address their questions and includes some general expectations, my choice of school supplies, time management ideas, sample weekly plans, and sample year plans.

General Expectations

When my students write, I encourage them to double-space their work — indeed, I expect them to do so. If they get into the habit of writing this way for all forms of writing, it makes the revision process much easier. The space provides room to insert words, phrases, or sentences, and makes it easier to change the order of sentences with arrows, brackets, and asterisks (all things you will demonstrate during the revision process). Although a seemingly simple expectation, it is one that will make the revision process easier to navigate.

Currently, I am writing and composing on the computer. There are times, though, when I prefer a notebook and pen.

A common question I receive: Do I expect printing, handwriting, or typed work? When they are writing creatively, I let my students choose their method. If what we truly value is the content of our students' work, the method should simply enhance the creative process. When you teach each form of writing, begin by having students compose on paper: printing or handwriting, whatever their preference. As you get to know your students, you may decide that some students need the computer even for the initial composition stage. Be open to this as this is a more accurate reflection of our society. If your students are writing a final draft, you might be more specific in the form you expect, but during the initial creative stage, respect the preferences of the individuals within your class.

For a final draft of student work, set the expectations early. During draft stages, I am not concerned about spelling, capitalization, punctuation, or even neatness. When a student submits a final draft, however, I have high expectations for quality of work. If you accept something for publication riddled with errors, you are sending a clear message about the quality of work you accept and setting yourself up for a year-long battle. Although we do not want students to worry about conventions during initial stages of writing, we do want them to meet high expectations for final drafts.

School Supplies

The use of particular school supplies is often an individual preference by the teacher and may also vary according to the grade level taught. For your reference, though, here is a summary of what I find most effective in my classroom for the various forms of writing.

- **Scribblers:** I use scribblers for four main purposes: (1) journal or weekend updates (see Chapter 5); (2) reader response (see Chapter 9); (3) author study (see Chapter 9); and (4) Writer's Workshop. For the latter use, students each have a designated scribbler where they can write whatever they choose. Most often they choose to write narrative stories, but this is a place for writing where they set the direction. If a student loves nonfiction, he or she may be writing expository text. Students can write in Writer's Workshop after they are finished other work or at given times throughout the week. Here they tend to try out various concepts we have been discussing — they get creative and enjoy experimenting with language. Sometimes, they bring something from their Writer's Workshop time to their individual writing conference.

- **A Visual Journal:** Each student in my class has one visual journal that we use in all subject areas. The visual journals I use are large coiled books of blank pages. The paper is heavier than your standard 20 lb weight. The entries in a visual journal are typically a combination of words and pictures. (For more detail, see Chapter 5.)

- **A Binder:** The binder is divided into four sections, each for a different kind of writing: (1) freewriting, (2) narrative writing, (3) transactional writing, and (4) poetry. At the beginning of the Freewriting section, my students keep a running list of the freewrites they complete. All freewrites are written on loose-leaf paper and kept in this section. Students add the date, the prompt/ title, and a brief comment to the list after each freewrite experience. They also write stories on loose-leaf paper so pages are easy to take in and out of the Narrative Writing section. They are not bound by a particular length as they are within a scribbler. With loose-leaf paper they can come back to a story they had started previously and add to it with ease (this practice will be discussed further in Chapter 6). Plot pattern graphic organizers can also be kept in this section for easy student reference. As for transactional writing and poetry, students can keep handouts as well as their pieces and poetry in the appropriate sections.

    Many teachers of primary grades prefer to use scribblers rather than binders, but I still recommend binders. When teaching these grades, I work up all of my courage and patience to teach the students how to use the binders properly at the beginning of the year — yes, step by step many times over; then, they get into the habit and the binders work beautifully. I won't deny it takes patience at the beginning, however.

With all grades, it is worth taking the time to walk through the organization of materials at the beginning of the year and then to hold students accountable for being organized on a continual basis. It develops routine and sets good habits.

Freewriting is discussed in Chapter 4, narrative writing in Chapter 6, transactional writing in Chapter 7, and poetry in Chapter 8.

Time Management

Another concern often voiced by teachers is time management. "How do I fit all of this writing into my timetable with so much curriculum to cover?" "How do I find the time?" These are reasonable questions: the answers lie in careful planning of the year, effective time management, and realistic approaches to assessment.

At the beginning of each year, I spend considerable time teaching the students my expectations. They know that when I ask them to take out a book, they are to do it immediately. When I ask them to get into their writing groups, they can do so within a minute. As much as possible, we don't lose instructional time during transitions. My students know that I mean business; they also know that they are in a lively classroom where curiosity, discovery, and fun are valued.

With some groups of students, management is relatively easy — they listen well and respond quickly — and yet, we have all had *that class* where classroom management requires more persistence and patience. If you are a new teacher or lucky enough that you have not yet had *that class*, your time will come. Regardless of the dynamics of your group, it is worth the effort at the beginning of the year to be insistent on immediate responses and effective use of time. The entire year will unfold more efficiently and be more fun for both you and your students.

The Benefits of Routine

To further capitalize on time, I establish routines: in fact, my students have specific expectations after each break in the day. For example, each Monday morning, my students write in their journals. Their journals are on their desks when they arrive and the students eagerly open them to read my responses or questions from last week. Once the routine is established, there is no need for instruction; they settle themselves into class, read my responses, and begin to write. It is a wonderful way to begin each week and within 30 minutes we are moving on to something else. Every other day of the week, the students anticipate what I call a "brain bender" at the beginning of the day (connected to curriculum in some way: usually a pre-reading activity). After lunch, we all pick up a good book.

Although they may not always admit it, children love routine. If you use it to your advantage, it can help you utilize your instructional time most effectively, minimize idle time, and set the tone for your community of learners. And though it will take some preplanning, it can make planning for the later part of the year much easier.

Time Spent Writing

As for the time spent writing, you are going to develop a routine and a rhythm in your own classroom. Although your students may be writing more than they have in the past, there are ways to find the time and also to make that time meaningful for them. As you will discover in Chapter 4, which focuses on freewriting, we write for only about five or six minutes at the beginning stages. The time slowly increases depending on the grade level, but it shouldn't be something that grows to an overwhelming amount. The longest freewrites with my Grade 6 classes are never more than 15 minutes. If students write longer than this during a freewrite, many of them find it challenging to keep their pencils moving and

On most occasions, freewrites are connected to the reading you are already doing within the classroom.

then you defeat the purpose. I would rather keep the time shorter and maintain positive attitudes towards the writing process.

Although time is spent teaching this method to our students initially, once established, the time is minimal and results in huge dividends. Typically, I plan my freewrite lessons to be 30 to 40 minutes. This includes both writing and sharing time.

The use of regular routines and careful planning will carve out time for other forms of writing in the classroom, as well. Journal writing and reader response will be completed once or twice weekly. Narrative writing and poetry can be units covered during the year. Typically, the editing, revising, and publishing stages take the most time. Fortunately, when we focus on the *process* of writing rather than the *product*, not everything our students write needs to be taken to a final stage. When we want them to edit and revise a piece of writing, they will have much to choose from. Since writing groups are established at the beginning of the year, they will not take much time to be effective.

As we will explore in other chapters, writing should occur within all curricular areas, not only language arts. Writing could occur in social studies after a conversation about our role in the community or the rights of a child. In science, students could write a journal entry or freewrite about how technologies such as airplanes or electricity have changed our world. In school districts with a religious mandate, writing could occur after a school-wide celebration or after a discussion about a parable. During math class, students could write about their strategies, struggles, or the steps involved in solving a problem. By writing often and in various subjects, our students will learn about audience and tone. Best of all, they will not only learn to write to communicate, but they will also learn that writing is a thought process connected to all disciplines. Through the process of writing we arrive at realizations and insights we might not otherwise consider. Therefore, our students should not only be learning to write, but also be writing to learn.

Time for Assessment?

Rest assured, though you and your students are writing frequently, not all of the writing needs to be assessed. In fact, it shouldn't be. You won't even be reading all of your students' writing. By writing often, your students will have some choice in what is assessed and, therefore, what you *are* assessing will typically be more interesting and enjoyable.

Weekly Plans

As a classroom teacher, I tend to follow a similar structure in language arts from week to week. This not only assists me with my planning, but it is also effective for students because they become accustomed to the routine in place.

Mentor Texts

When I plan my week in language arts, I use a mentor text to guide my teaching. A mentor text can be anything from a picture book to a selection from an anthology to a novel. Regardless of the form, I use the mentor text(s) to teach my concepts for the week. I continually intertwine our reading and writing.

In addition to choosing reading selections for the concept I am planning to teach, I look for mentor texts that reflect the students in my class. By looking for diverse books that represent various cultures, we add a further dimension to our teaching. It is important to consider our students when choosing our mentor texts.

In my recent schools, we have had many students of African descent. To ensure that the students can relate to the texts, I incorporate books representing their culture. This idea was reinforced when I visited a Grade 3 class in my school during Read In Week. A little boy in that class had arrived in Canada from Sudan the previous year. When he came to us, he spoke no English. One of the books I brought to share with the class was *Me … Jane* by Patrick McDonnell. Well, when I read the word *Africa*, did he ever perk up and listen! In fact, he interjected while I was reading, and we engaged in a quick discussion about Sudan.

Mentor Texts with a Cultural Component

- *The Boy Who Harnessed the Wind: Creating Currents of Electricity and Hope* by William Kamkwamba and Bryan Mealer
- *Four Feet, Two Sandals* by Karen Lynn Williams and Khadra Mohammed
- *Freedom Summer* by Deborah Wiles
- *Goal!* by Mina Javaherbin
- *Hope Springs* by Eric Walters
- *Lost and Found Cat: The True Story of Kunkush's Incredible Journey* by Doug Kuntz and Amy Shrodes
- *My Name Is Blessing* by Eric Walters
- *The Name Jar* by Yangsook Choi
- *One Green Apple* by Eve Bunting
- *The Orphan Boy* by Tololwa M. Mollel
- *Stepping Stones: A Refugee Family's Journey* by Margriet Ruurs
- *Today Is the Day* by Eric Walters
- *The Water Princess* by Susan Verde

In addition to there being many excellent picture books, Nelson publishes several series that celebrate the Indigenous peoples of Canada: *Nelson Literacy Storytelling Kit* and the *Circle of Life Series*.

Another group of students to consider is our Indigenous population. We now recognize that our Indigenous students have been treated substantially different than most. With residential schools behind us, it is important to include and represent Indigenous students in our classrooms. When we feature mentor texts reflecting this culture, our Indigenous students will be able to see themselves represented and valued in society.

Mentor Texts Representing the Indigenous Population

- *Cloudwalker* by Roy Henry Vickers and Robert Budd
- *The Elders Are Watching* by David Bouchard
- *The First Mosquito* by Caroll Simpson
- *I Am Not a Number* by Jenny Kay Dupuis and Kathy Kacer
- *Orca Chief* by Roy Henry Vickers and Robert Budd
- *Raven Brings the Light* by Roy Henry Vickers and Robert Budd
- *SkySisters* by Jan Bourdeau Waboose

Sample Plan

In my sample weekly plan, which provides a structure to my week, you will notice references to various forms of writing. These forms are outlined in detail in subsequent chapters.

Sample Weekly Plan

Monday
- Begin the day with a journal entry. I have the journals waiting on the students' desks when they come into class. They look forward to my responses from last week and then begin to write. I do this every Monday without fail.
- Hold three or four individual writing conferences as students are writing in their journals. (Chapter 3 discusses this in detail.)
- Introduce vocabulary words for the week. We discuss any patterns that the students notice in the group of words. I choose my words intentionally to ensure that there is some pattern: for example, words from the same family, words with prefixes, or compound words.
- Make predictions. Students are asked to brainstorm and predict what the vocabulary words have in common and therefore what the mentor text might be about.

Tuesday
- I have a pre-reading activity for the mentor text ready for students when they enter the classroom on Tuesday morning. It might be a brainstorm activity, a personal connection to a topic, or even a prediction. My goal for this pre-reading activity is to activate my students' background knowledge about the topic.
- Once students are given the text, I encourage them to look for the vocabulary words from yesterday. In time, they do this naturally without me initiating the task.
- Next, we complete our first reading of the mentor text selection. Most often we do this first reading together as a whole group. Sometimes, it is done in partners and sometimes alone (with guided reading for those who need it). This decision is made based on the difficulty of the text and my purpose for the lesson.
- Our discussion about reading strategies is embedded in the lesson whenever possible.
- After reading, we engage in discussion about the text, assessing the accuracy of our predictions, and sometimes we complete a post-reading activity.

Wednesday
- We begin the day with the rereading of the mentor text selection. Again, I vary how we read the text: sometimes, I read aloud to the whole group; sometimes, students read in partners; and sometimes, they read alone (with support for those who need it).
- I teach a mini-lesson related to the mentor text.
- We engage in discussion about what we understood better after reading the selection a second time through.
- There is a post-reading activity, possibly grammar, writing, reader response, reflection, or discussion.

Thursday
- We begin the morning with a freewrite (sometimes two) connected to the reading selection.
- After writing, we share our freewrites.

- After three or four freewrites in consecutive weeks, the students choose one to take to their writing group for further work.
- If we are not working in writing groups this week, we would do another post-reading activity.

Friday
- We finish up with a vocabulary lesson and word work.
- The class is introduced to other texts or genres somehow connected to the mentor text. Sometimes, I read these to the students; sometimes, I provide options for the students to read on their own.
- Students continue work with freewriting or post-reading activities.

This is my general structure for planning my week. As you are learning the structure, begin by choosing selections from an anthology. These are typically accompanied by a teacher's guide that will provide appropriate pre-reading and post-reading activities. As you become more comfortable with the structure of the week, you will be able to choose a picture book for a mentor text and then determine your own pre-reading and post-reading activities more easily.

Year Plans

It is difficult to provide a specific year plan for you at your grade level as the curriculum varies across the country. However, in an exploration of the language curriculums across Canada, I noted that most focus on six language processes in some form or another: speaking, listening, reading, writing, viewing, and representing. These strands, or processes, tend to be the foundation for language arts curriculums. Although this book is primarily about the teaching of writing, the other five strands are interwoven throughout it. One process cannot be entirely separate from the other.

There are three important forms of writing to establish quite soon within your classroom: freewriting, journal writing, and reader response. These should be established at the beginning of the year and continue throughout the year (see Chapters 4, 5, and 9). I also establish writing groups early in the year: the sooner this becomes an expectation and a habit within your classroom, the more effective the groups will be.

I have included two sample year plans for your reference. You can adjust this year plan as necessary for both your grade level and your specific curriculum. Notice that students are both *learning to writing* and *writing to learn* in each month of the school year. Bear in mind that these plans are guidelines only.

Sample Plan: Grade 1

Grade 1 is a unique year because students are truly beginning writers. For this reason, the sample year plan is different than the others. (Chapter 11 is specific to the realities of teaching writing to these emergent writers.)

I have not included a year plan for Kindergarten. Much of the information on the year plans from Grades 1 to 6 is simply not covered in the Kindergarten curriculum. For details about writing in Kindergarten, see Chapter 11.

Month	Introduce ...	Related Skills	Continue With ...
September	Daily phonics Journal writing	Invented spelling High-frequency words Finger spacing Capital letters Basic punctuation	
October	Reader response (earlier if the group is ready) Visual journals	Responding to texts: making connections	Daily phonics Journal writing
November	Narrative writing (transformation stories) Letter writing: Letter to Santa	Beginning, middle, end Varied sentence beginnings	Daily phonics Journal writing Reader response Visual journals
December	Narrative writing (transformation stories)	Beginning, middle, end Character development	Daily phonics Journal writing Reader response Visual journals
January	Freewriting Expository	Ideas and content Organization Text features	Daily phonics Journal writing Reader response Visual journals
February	Narrative writing (stuck stories) Writing groups	Organization Revising, editing	Daily phonics Journal writing Reader response Visual journals Freewriting
March	Letter writing (continued) Opinion pieces	Writing for an authentic audience	Journal writing Reader response Visual journals Freewriting Writing groups
April	Poetry	Similes, metaphor, hyperbole, personification, alliteration, rhythm, rhyme	Journal writing Reader response Visual journals Freewriting Writing groups
May	Narrative writing	Character development Setting	Journal writing Reader response Visual journals Freewriting Writing groups
June	Author study	Responding to texts: making connections, comparisons	Journal writing Reader response Visual journals Freewriting Writing groups

Sample Plan: Grades 2 to 6

I tend to follow a similar language arts plan no matter what grade level I teach. The plan below highlights when I introduce the various forms of writing throughout the school year. I have included some of the related skills, but there are so many I could not include them all.

Month	Introduce ...	Related Skills	Continue With ...
September	Freewriting Journal writing Reader response Writing groups	Ideas and content Responding to texts: making connections, comparisons Revision, editing conventions	
October	Visual journals (earlier, if time allows) Expository	Sentence fluency Text features	Freewriting Journal writing Reader response Writing groups
November	Letter writing Narrative writing (transformation stories)	Beginning, middle, end Organization Character development	Freewriting Journal writing Reader response Writing groups Visual journals
December	Narrative writing (transformation stories)	Character development	Freewriting Journal writing Reader response Writing groups Visual journals
January	Narrative writing (stuck stories)	Dialogue Setting	Freewriting Journal writing Reader response Writing groups Visual journals
February	Opinion and persuasive pieces Grades 5 & 6: Article writing	Fact and opinion Writing for an authentic audience	Freewriting Journal writing Reader response Writing groups Visual journals
March	Narrative writing (Choose between circle stories, competition stories, or quest stories.)	Organization Ideas and content	Freewriting Journal writing Reader response Writing groups Visual journals

April	Poetry	Rhythm, rhyme, similes, metaphor, hyperbole, personification, alliteration, onomatopoeia (Choose according to grade-level curriculum.)	Freewriting Journal writing Reader response Writing groups Visual journals
May	Expository Narrative writing (student choice for plot patterns)	Text features Specific skills needed most by your group of students	Freewriting Journal writing Reader response Writing groups Visual journals
June	Author study	Responding to texts: making connections, comparisons	Freewriting Journal writing Reader response Writing groups Visual journals

The Challenges of Planning Language Arts

In most subjects we teach, the knowledge-based content guides our planning; however, language arts is a skills-based curriculum. Because of that, many teachers have voiced their frustrations and challenges in planning the year.

The suggestions in this chapter are based on my own trial and error over the years. There is no such thing as a one-size-fits-all approach. Even within my own classroom, I vary my typical year plans and weekly plans to suit the needs of my students and the scheduling constraints within my school. So, you will have to find the year plan, time management strategies, and school supplies that work best for you and your students. Consider this chapter a starting point!

3

Creating a Healthy Attitude towards Assessment

"Not everything that matters can be measured, and not everything that is measured matters."
— Elliot Eisner

Assessment is sometimes considered a necessary evil. Some teachers use assessment punitively and, therefore, their students cringe at every assessment they receive. And yet, we can teach our students to view assessment as an opportunity for improvement. Our own views of assessment as teachers will influence the way assessment is viewed by the students in our classrooms.

The Gift of Perspective

As with each of us, my own views of assessment have been guided by my experiences. Generally, I was a good student in school. I do however have a vivid recollection of my first failing grade. It was a Grade 5 French test. I do not recall the mark itself, but I do remember the feelings of defeat and embarrassment when I saw the score on that test. I remember walking home from school, contemplating how to tell my parents. I remember entering the house and my mother immediately asking, "What's wrong?" I also remember her response: "It's only one test."

That day, as we sat on the steps of the back porch, tears streaming down my face, my mother gave me the gift of perspective: perspective I didn't have as a young student dealing with the sometimes harsh realities of assessment. And although it probably wasn't my only poor grade during my education, that particular incident has stayed with me.

I now feel fortunate that I was able to experience the range of emotions tied to assessment. I have come to realize the power of assessment and the impact it can have on our students. Because of that experience, I can better empathize with and understand those students who regularly receive those grades, sometimes despite their best efforts.

The reality is, just like you, I have taught many students during my career who work very hard and simply cannot achieve at grade level: students who become accustomed to failing grades. I have also witnessed parents telling their children that the 90 percent on that test is not good enough. Therefore, it is vital that we as teachers become the perspective that my mother was for me.

"It's Only One Test"

We must engage in conversations about strengths, challenges, and learning styles to help our students develop a healthy perspective towards assessment. We simply do not know what our students hear at home or even what their internal dialogue might be. My mom's response to me when I was a young student — "It's only one test" — speaks to an important reality of assessment. Assessments are snapshots of a student's understanding in a particular moment, under those particular circumstances.

How do we maintain a realistic emphasis on assessment within our classrooms? How do we ensure that assessment does not dampen our students' enthusiasm for learning? How do we use assessment as an opportunity for growth?

To begin, I suggest discussing these questions with your students:

- Why do we have assessment?
- What are the different methods of assessment?
- How can assessments be helpful to us as learners?
- How does it make you feel when I assess your work?
- What makes the process of assessment easier for you?

Their responses will help you to gauge their existing attitudes towards assessment, allowing you to guide the conversation appropriately. The earlier you have these conversations, the better.

Most important, encourage your students to view assessment as a tool for self-improvement. Teach them that assessment is not a competition between students but a way to challenge each of them to do their best work. Remind them that few of us are good at everything and that we all have our own strengths and passions. Dialogue openly with your students, whatever their age. The work you have done to establish a positive community of learners will pay its dividends and help create a healthy attitude towards assessment.

"Classrooms are places of genuine learning when children and teachers can consider the classroom to be OurSpace. This ownership of space includes negotiation of assessment practices and standards." — Jill Kedersha McClay and Margaret Mackey (2009, 126–27)

Be Constructive, Not Punitive

When you assess your students' assignments, be cognizant of what you write on their work. A large, dark *D* scrawled at the top of the page can be humiliating. Comments such as "You can do better!" or "Disappointing!" can be discouraging to even our most confident students. Even if that student *could* do better, we can support learning and maintain self-esteem by writing more appropriate comments. In elementary schools, the goals of our assessments should be to determine a current level of achievement and assist our students in improving. Even if the assessment is summative and we will not be returning to the topic, we are wise to pay heed to the tone of our comments.

For the most part, assessment in language arts tends to be formative and ongoing throughout the year. On the other hand, skills in mathematics — such as fractions or measurement, for instance — are typically taught during a particular unit and then not revisited again during the school year. The same is true for most of the content in subjects like social studies or science. Reading and writing, however, are skills we focus on throughout the entire school year and also from year to year. In both reading and writing, assessments identify areas of strength and weakness and help us guide future learning.

That was not how it was when I was a student in the classroom, however. I would hand in a written assignment and get it back with a grade. Rarely did I have the opportunity to improve what I was doing. I would have loved to receive feedback during the writing process in order to know how to make what I was working on better.

I had a special opportunity for feedback when I was a Grade 9 student. I remember the incident vividly. I had been chosen to give a speech at our Grade 9 graduation. I was asked to take a draft copy to one of our teachers for discussion. The time I spent with him was immensely productive. In those moments, he taught me about parallel structure and its impact. I still think about his words today.

Assessment for Learning

What made that time with him so memorable? Well, it was authentic: I was writing for a real purpose and an authentic audience. What's more, it was timely. It wasn't about a grade for my report card but about making my writing the best it could be for an upcoming event. Little did I know then that the lesson went far beyond parallel structure: that experience became the model for the writing conferences that I engage in with my students. The teacher taught me about *assessment for learning* long before I was a teacher in the classroom.

To keep assessment in my classroom appropriate and reasonable, I do not assess everything my students write. Over-assessment robs our students of the freedom that allows them to take risks and become competent, creative individuals. My students know beforehand that they will pick one of every three or four pieces of writing to be assessed. Therefore, they do not worry about being assessed as they are writing. They are also not yet worried about someone reading their work. If they decide to use a particular piece of writing for an assessment, they know they will have time to revisit it before it is handed in. Not only can they choose the writing that will be assessed, but they also have the opportunity to assess their work before I do and to write a short reflection about it.

If you have been focusing on one area of writing such as sentence fluency or word choice, assess your students' work *only* for this component. Consider how much time you will save, still accomplishing what you need to accomplish! I also allow the students to be involved in the assessment process by assisting me in the creation of rubrics for specific projects we might be working on. All of these factors help students to work more productively and creatively without the worry of a looming grade.

When my students write in subjects other than language arts, the writing is not typically assessed. If this writing is truly writing to understand, or *writing to learn*, then there is no need for the students to receive a grade. If, for some reason, I do decide to assess the work, the students are involved in the process and know specifically what they will be assessed on.

Best of all, my students' writing has become so interesting that I look forward to reading it. The students also look forward to sharing their work. When a student exclaims, "Listen to how this sounds!" I know I am in for a good piece of writing; this student has obviously given much thought to her writing and is proud of her work.

There are three forms of assessment essential for student improvement in the area of writing: (1) rubrics, (2) conferencing, and (3) reflection and goal setting.

Rubrics

The 6 + 1 Traits of Writing model focuses on seven qualities that define good writing: ideas, organization, voice, word choice, sentence fluency, conventions, and presentation. Ruth Culham authored several highly recommended books to guide both instruction and assessment practices:
- *6 + 1 Traits of Writing: The Complete Guide for the Primary Grades*
- *6 + 1 Traits of Writing: The Complete Guide, Grades 3 and Up*

Rubrics are my primary form of summative assessment for writing, but they should also be used throughout the process as formative assessment. I often utilize the 6 + 1 Trait rubrics for writing and I highly recommend them. In addition, though, I have developed rubrics targeted to various types of writing (these are included in each of the appropriate chapters). Building rubrics with students is also an effective endeavor. It can be somewhat time-consuming but valuable for students given how much time they will work with the rubric. By developing the rubric together, they know exactly what the criteria are for their work.

Regardless of whether the rubric is class created or provided by the teacher, students should get to know it well. Students should always have the opportunity to refer to the rubrics during the writing and revision stages as a guide to improve their work. "Then the target is visible — and thus much easier to hit" (Spandel 2001, 5).

One of the most important benefits of rubrics is the common language they provide. As Vicki Spandel (2001) notes, "How different writing instruction — and assessment — can be when teachers and their students share a common vocabulary that allows them to think, speak, assess, and plan like writers. Suddenly, there is no more mystery" (xiii). This common language is used during mini-lessons, conferencing, and writing group sessions.

Use of Rubrics within Writing Groups

In fact, one strategy I have found effective is to give the rubric to the students to discuss in their writing groups. They can explore and talk about the various criteria for each category. Once you have developed a strong community of learners, students can bring a piece of writing and the rubric to their groups for discussion. Students can learn to respectfully discuss each other's work as part of the process of formative assessment. Modelling these discussions is important to ensure that students do not belittle their peers, either purposely or inadvertently.

This conversation surrounding assessment becomes a critical process in the improvement of student writing. Gone are the days of students writing and handing in what they have written without the opportunity for improvement. With rubrics as a target, peer- and self-assessment, and discussion during writing groups, students will revisit their work and revise. This process naturally yields stronger writing.

Conferencing

A powerful form of formative assessment is conferencing. I have a short writing conference with each of my students once a month. I use the time when most students are journal writing, narrative writing, or even engaged in quiet reading to meet with an individual student. I purposely keep the time short (about five minutes per student) because I know that I have a classroom full of writers who need my attention. We simply meet at my desk or the back table and talk through the writing. Sometimes, the writer begins by reading a portion of his or her work out loud to me. Other times I begin with an open-ended question or statement: "Tell me about your writing." Calkins and Martinelli (2006) emphasize the importance of waiting for the writer to answer:

Don't underestimate the importance of silence. When I ask the question, "What are you working on today as a writer?" it is critical that I actually sit there and wait for a length of time that communicates to the children that it's their job to fill the silence with real thinking. (40)

For the remainder of the conference, I may have noted something to discuss (e.g., organization, details, conventions) but I always give the student time to ask me specific questions. Because they know this is the routine, as the months go on, they look forward to the conference and often come to me with specific, prepared questions about their writing.

If I have scheduled conferences with Jenna, Tom, and Liz tomorrow, I might leave a note on their desks as a reminder. This is their cue to review their writing and begin thinking about what they want to discuss. They can look through their recent freewrites or narrative writing and then be more prepared for our conference. Again, this is a routine that you establish in your class.

> **Even though I am sometimes conferencing during the time students are writing in their journals, we do not conference *about* their journals. I keep journal writing as a form of writing completely without judgment or assessment.**

Possible Questions or Comments for Conferences

- What did you bring to me today? Why did you choose this piece of writing?
- Tell me about your writing.
- How do you feel about this piece of writing so far?
- Are you finished or are you planning to add more?
- What else could you add to make this piece more effective?
- Is there anything you are struggling with or wondering about?
- I didn't understand what you meant here … Could you tell me more?
- Tell me about your beginning section. Are you happy with it? Do you think there is anything you could do to make it more effective?
- Tell me more about your main character.
- Who is your audience?
- Have you given your work a title? Explain what you're thinking.
- Why did you choose this piece of writing to bring to a final stage?
- What questions do you have about your writing?
- Do you think this writing was inspired by something you heard or saw?

Individual conferencing is useful to guide students during the next month of writing. After our short literary discussion, I encourage students to develop a goal. I provide guidance and prompting with this as necessary.

I use a line master like the one on page 36 to record the notes of our conference. I make one page for each student in my class.

Reflection and Goal Setting

As part of the assessment process, students must have time for reflection and goal setting. These practices are an important part of our students' learning and development. Reflections can periodically be built into regular journal-writing time. Try these simple but effective prompts:

- I know I am an effective student when …
- This week, my greatest learning was …

- I would like to become better at …
- I have become very good at …

Our writing conferences also include time for reflection and goal setting. When we teach our students to reflect on their own learning, students begin to see how they have ownership in the learning process.

To assist students with their processes of reflection and goal setting, it can be helpful for them to see samples of work from various points in the year. Prompt them to look through writing scribblers, a section of their binder, or a portfolio that has monthly samples. Guide their reflection further by asking students to take notice of something in particular. If, for example, you have been focusing on word choice, ask them to examine their writing for interesting words. This kind of direction often leads to a personal goal that, in turn, makes students more cognizant of word choice in daily writing. This reflection process works for many skills, such as varying sentence length, making proper use of punctuation, and organizing ideas.

Through this process students are empowered to take ownership of their learning and to strive for their personal best.

Assess to Promote Learning

Although assessment is a necessary and purposeful part of our job as educators, it should be used carefully and intentionally to provide feedback for improvement. The focus becomes assessment *for* learning, rather than assessment *of* learning. The students in my class come to expect to be thinking about their thinking, writing about their writing, and talking about their talking. If we have established a community of learners, assessment will be an accepted and practical component of our classrooms used to promote growth and learning. Our students should feel comfortable enough in our classrooms to take risks and know that making mistakes is acceptable: they should come to realize that through this process the greatest learning transpires.

This chapter provides general strategies for the assessment of writing. I have also included a section about assessment in several of the subsequent chapters to provide more explicit information about the specific content.

Student–Teacher Conference Notes

Student Name:			
Date	**Teacher Initiated**	**Student Concerns**	**Student Goal**
September _____			
October _____			
November _____			
December _____			
January _____			
February _____			
March _____			
April _____			
May _____			
June _____			

Pembroke Publishers © 2017 *How Do I Get Them to Write?* by Karen Filewych ISBN 978-1-55138-322-4

4
Freewriting

"To gain your own voice, you have to forget about having it heard."
— Allen Ginsberg

With no other genre or writing process have I been able to uncover my students' voices as with freewriting. Without the time to censor their thoughts, students tend to write with honesty and heart: thus, their voices begin to emerge through their work.

Despite the grade level I teach, I write with my students at least two or three times a week in a method called "freewriting." Peter Elbow popularized this method of writing several decades ago. "Freewriting is the easiest way to get words on paper and the best all-around practice in writing that I know" (Elbow 1998, 13). I agree wholeheartedly. Freewrites are short, timed periods where our pens or pencils or fingers on the keyboard do not stop. No rereading, stopping, crossing out, or fixing up at this stage. No censoring. No worrying about an audience. No worrying about spelling or grammar or punctuation. What freedom! And typically, much different from the way our students have previously been taught. Yet freewriting can produce raw and convincing work. As John Trimble writes:

> Remember, many of your best ideas are probably lurking in your unconscious. If you slow down to edit what you've written, you'll put an airtight lid on those unconscious thoughts and begin experiencing that agonizing "blocked" feeling that we're all familiar with. (1975, 11)

I don't typically tell my students how long we will write during a freewrite. I begin with about five minutes but then I gauge how long to write when I see how involved the students are with the particular prompt. If many seem to be slowing down, I may stop after six or seven minutes. If they seem to be especially engaged, we persist for a few more minutes. My students know not go to the bathroom or sharpen a pencil or talk to their neighbor during a freewrite: everyone writes the entire time. This expectation is set from the first time we freewrite and we never deviate. You may be surprised to see students rise to this challenge.

Freeing First Thoughts

I always remind students that at this point, it is about the process, not the end product. *After* writing, they will have the opportunity to revise and edit, but not *during*.

When first learning to do freewrites, it can be difficult for some writers to keep their pens or pencils moving. The trick is to rewrite the prompt anytime the hand stops moving. For example, if the prompt is "I love to …," some students may be able to write and keep writing the whole time. Some, however, especially as they first learn the process, will be tempted to stop to reread their work, and others will be tempted to stop entirely, claiming they have nothing more to write about. By writing the prompt again (and again and again, if necessary), they will learn to continue writing. It truly doesn't matter if they have three sentences in a row beginning with the prompt. Eventually, they will expand on their ideas rather than rewrite the prompt sentence.

Consider this: if we thought every word we spoke had to be dazzling and impressive, how much would we speak? So, too, with our writing. The pressure of knowing our work is to be read and the self-expectation for immediate perfection can be a stumbling block to good writing and sometimes to any writing at all. We can always revise once we have words on the page. Pulitzer Prize–winning novelist James A. Michener once said, "I have never thought of myself as a good writer. Anyone who wants reassurance of that should read one of my first drafts. But I'm one of the world's great rewriters." I have taught freewriting for years. With most classes, the response has been immediately positive and productive. With others, it took a few experiences for the students to become comfortable.

Perhaps the most important part of this process is that I freewrite with my students. Students are much more willing to make themselves vulnerable through writing when they see their teacher doing the same. By our writing together, students see the process in action. They also come to understand that writing is something that we (students and teacher alike) can do to explore our thoughts and extend our learning in any subject. You may be skeptical of the process if you are not naturally a writer yourself. However, by writing, too, you become much more invested in the process and more understanding of the experience for your students.

Who makes the better physical education teacher: the one who dresses the part and demonstrates and participates with the students, or the one wearing the skirt and high heels, standing on the sideline telling the students what to do? A stereotype maybe, but grounded in truth. Students appreciate the participation of the teacher in any subject.

You may be surprised at the many benefits you experience when writing with your students. You will begin to relate to what they experience during writing and be able to say, "When I was writing …" or "Here's how I'm planning to revise …" You will likely become more sensitive during the process of assessment, too. And most important, by making yourself vulnerable during the writing process, you are leading by example, and you will come to understand the feeling of vulnerability experienced by many of your students.

After each freewrite, I ask for volunteers to read their writing out loud. The students can choose to read none, some, or all of their work to the class; they also know that I have the same choice. The students become more confident reading their work out loud because everyone clearly understands that the work is only a first draft. After all, we have just watched each other spend only about seven minutes on this piece of writing. Before long, students who have never volunteered to read their writing out loud begin to volunteer. A gleam appears in their eyes as we spend the minute or two after a freewrite quietly reading over our own work.

What about the poor spelling and grammar and lack of punctuation? As Tony Stead (2002) observes, "For some, spelling words correctly becomes the focus of their writing, and getting across the information … becomes secondary" (71–72). By teaching our students the process of freewriting, we *free* them from worrying about spelling (or anything else) during writing. We teach students that the focus is on the process, not yet the end result.

Writing with Your Students

While students are writing in their journals or doing narrative writing, I am typically conferencing with individuals or checking in on student progress. Only during freewriting do I engage in the writing process. I would encourage you to do the same. Every time. No exceptions. It certainly gets easier the more you do it, and students will appreciate your efforts.

A Choice among Freewrites

When I ask students to choose one of the last four or five freewrites to take to a published level, they search through, reread, and become excited about their choice. They then spend time reworking, reshaping, adding, deleting, and, of course, editing. Best of all, they do this willingly!

The Emergence of Voice

I have engaged in this process with students as young as Grade 1. The change in writing is inspiring. The quality of writing changes from dull and repetitive to inventive and interesting to read. The students begin to write from a place of emotion rather than purely from the intellect. It is often through the process of freewriting that we begin to hear the *voice* of our student writers coming through. Just as those who know us recognize our speaking voice — our inflections, tone, intonation, cadence, volume, and even our diction choices — our writing, too, should have a strong voice that enables the reader to recognize that profoundly human and authentic part of us. In *Writing Down the Bones*, Natalie Goldberg (1986) discusses this type of writing:

> The aim is to burn through to first thoughts, to the place where energy is unobstructed by social politeness or the internal censor, to the place where you are writing what your mind actually sees and feels, not what it *thinks* it should see or feel. (8)

Freewriting begins to reveal more of their person, their thought patterns, their perspectives, and their perceptions.

When freewriting with your class, be persistent and celebrate small successes. It is certainly worth the effort: through this process, students often become amazed at what they can write. Another beauty of the process is that it tends to provide all students with an opportunity for success despite the range of ability levels among them.

If you are a teacher who enjoys writing, I recommend reading *Writing Down the Bones* by Natalie Goldberg and *Bird by Bird* by Anne Lamott. These books will guide and inspire your own writing, and ultimately, assist you as a teacher of writing.

Freewriting as the Backbone of the Writing Program

Though I do teach the writing process, freewriting is the backbone of my program. In essence, I often use freewriting as the drafting or planning stage. This allows my students to get to the meat of the topic or to explore their emotions and beliefs. The revision stage and the work within writing groups then allows for further brainstorming, reorganization, or the addition of details as necessary. Freewriting liberates our student writers, and they begin to look forward to writing rather than dreading it. Reluctant writers, no more!

How to Introduce a Freewrite

The first experience with a freewrite is an important one. This initial lesson will likely take 45 minutes or so. Once freewrites are established they take very little time. Invest the time up front to ensure that they are effective.

Begin by asking your students if they enjoy writing. There are always some that do! For those that say no, explore their reasons. What is it they don't like? Typically, they will touch on the following ideas: they have nothing to write about, they are not good writers, they don't know how to spell, they don't want anyone to read their work.

After this discussion, introduce the idea of a freewrite. Talk about how this process can lessen some of their anxiety about writing because they don't have to worry about perfect spelling or punctuation. Explain that they will be in control over whether someone reads their work: they will have the option of reading all, some, or none of their work on any given day. I explain that something might feel too personal to share and that's okay. This concept alone makes freewriting much less intimidating to students.

After this discussion — a vital one to set up freewrites effectively — begin writing. Spend five or six minutes writing in the style of a freewrite. The time is fluid based on the prompt and the students' response to the prompt. Each time you engage in a freewrite, judge the length of writing time based on the engagement of the class. If they are still writing, persist a little longer. If they seem to be slowing down, give the minute warning. Remind students that we do not stop our pen, pencil, or fingers on the keyboard. We simply write. One of the easiest prompts to begin with is "I remember ..."

When your students are freewriting, be sure you are writing too. If this evokes fear in you, as it does for many teachers, consider how your students feel when you ask them to write. When they see you engage in this behavior, it will help ease their fears.

Usually with about a minute left for writing, I quietly say, "Okay, class, finish your thoughts and then read your work to yourself."

Once all of us have read over our own work, I invite students to read some or all of their work to the class. On the first day especially, I try to share a portion of my work even if it's just a sentence or two. Modelling this helps set the stage for all future sharing.

A Non-threatening Discussion

Let's say I have used the prompt "I remember ..." I might show my students how I have written about three separate topics within our writing time. The first section was about the day I got my dog. The second section was the first day I started work at our school. The third section was about the day my father died. By explaining this to them, I can show how some of my writing is too personal to share. Therefore, I might share only the one section about my dog. By explaining how I wrote about three topics, I can also have a discussion about how I might later revise this work. "If I were to take this work to a published level, would it make sense to use all three paragraphs about such diverse topics?" They quickly realize that I would revise to focus on one topic. I explain how I might take one of the topics and write about it further. Today's writing could be the starting point, but I can later add to it and take out the parts that are irrelevant to the topic.

As you can see, this becomes a very natural discussion about revision. What's more, because we are discussing *my* work, the students find it non-threatening. They begin to see how the process of freewriting is liberating. Was it wrong that I wrote about three topics? Not at all. It was simply what came to mind when I was writing. My goal was to keep my pen moving.

When it comes to reading aloud to the class, you, too, will have the option of reading none, some, or all of your writing.

Do not give up if freewriting is not magical the first time: persist. However, the teachers I know who have tried this method are pleasantly surprised at the outcome even after the first attempt.

When to Use Freewrites

- Some of the most powerful writing from my students has stemmed from free-writes immediately after a shared reading. Connect your freewrites to a story, article, or poem you have read with your class. For example, consider the topics of child labor, place, peace, anger, and love. Many of the classroom anthologies have excellent poems, passages, or stories that can become writing prompts.
- On some occasions before a freewrite, engage the class in a lively discussion or debate about a given topic; then, abruptly stop the debate and let the writing begin. Return to the discussion after your writing time to see what new ideas emerge.
- As you will see in upcoming chapters, I recommend using freewrites as a warm-up or brainstorming for other genres of writing. For example, students will write about setting or characters and then use the details in their narrative stories.
- You can also use freewrites as a response to a video, guest speaker, or presentation; after a field trip; after a walk or physical education class; and outside surrounded by nature.

Effective Prompts

- Whenever possible, provide a simple prompt of about two or three words. Here is a basic list of common effective prompts focused on *I*:

I remember …	I want …	I collect …
I am …	I need …	I like to …
I am not …	I think …	I'm afraid of …
I've lost …	I feel …	Sometimes, I dream …

- Sometimes, offer prompts with slightly longer sentence starters, such as these:

I want to be …	If I could go anywhere in the world …
I'm worried about …	What I like best about this class is …
I'm not afraid of …	If I could choose another name, I'd
I wish my parents knew …	choose …
I feel good when …	The funniest thing I ever saw …
I don't like people who …	When I was six …
I'm proud of myself when …	The best laugh I've heard is …
	You won't believe this, but …

- Students might respond to a prompt such as "A friend is …" or "My family is …"
- Sometimes, students can write about something more outside themselves, as in "Everybody should …" or "The trouble with …"
- Consider inviting students to write about favorites: My favorite food is …, My least favorite food is …, My favorite animal is …
- Let students write based on a person of your choice or theirs: My mom …, My dad …, My sister …, My brother …, My grandmother …, My uncle …
- Choose a word, either concrete or abstract, for everyone to write about on the same day: love, hope, happiness, sadness, Christmas, summer, money, pain, school, home.

- Put a provocative statement on the board, for example, "Every school should hire a police officer" or "Dogs are better than cats." Have students address the topic, responding with "I agree ..." or "I disagree ..."
- Invite students to complete the following sentence and write about it further: "There are not enough _____ in the world."
- Provide a sensory writing experience. The students can write about popcorn while watching and listening to it pop, while smelling it and perhaps even tasting it. "Popcorn is ..."
- Give an *If* prompt. For example: If children ruled the world ..., If I could fly ..., If I were the principal ..., If my dog could talk ..., If I had a magic wand ..., If we ran out of water ..., If I had to move next week ...
- Once your class becomes familiar with the idea of freewrites, offer a visual prompt. To prepare, collect interesting pictures or items. You could show your older students a dramatic news photo. For younger students, try something intriguing or perhaps a tad bizarre. For instance, I have used a picture of a clutch of ducks swimming in a bathroom sink or another of a cat playing with a Rubik's Cube.
- Arrange for students to write to music. You might try Vivaldi, Mozart, or Handel. Try Oscar Peterson, *The Phantom of the Opera*, or Enya. Afterwards, discuss the differences in the students' writing process and product when they write to music. This approach is especially effective with simple two-word prompts such as "I feel ...," "I need ...," "I think ...," "I remember ...," "I am ..."
- For an interesting twist, have the class write two freewrite opposites one after the other. For example, spend six or seven minutes writing "I'm afraid of ..." and then surprise the students and have them spend six or seven more minutes writing "I'm not afraid of ..." Other pairs of prompts that work well include "I want ..." and "I need ..."; "I love ..." and "I hate ..."; and "I know ..." and "I don't know ..."

Feedback in Writing Groups

After four or five freewrites, ask students to choose one of their recent freewrites to read to their writing group. Encourage them to read their pieces of choice to themselves at their desks before they join their group. At this time, they can fix little mistakes, such as repeated words, lack of punctuation, and incorrect spelling — things they may not have noticed when they first wrote the piece. (For the set-up of writing groups, see Chapter 2.) When students enter their writing groups for the first few times, I give them a prompt page to take with them.

Prompt pages are visuals that guide the groups' oral discussion.

Initially, the feedback to their peers can be given orally; however, as they become more comfortable giving feedback, I provide them with feedback strips, one for each member of the group, on which they can write feedback to their peers. They fill out a feedback strip as or after each writer reads a piece of work aloud. The writers then take these strips back to their desks and staple them to the freewrite page that they just read to the group. I always give them time after meeting with their writing group to work on edits and revisions.

Sample Feedback Strips

```
Writer: _____ Listener: _____ Date: _____

This reminded me of …



I want to hear more about …



I was confused about …



```

```
Writer: _____ Listener: _____ Date: _____

I like the sound of …



I want to hear more about …



While you read, I remembered/I felt …



```

Assessment: Reflection for Improvement

From time to time, I ask my students to complete a more in-depth reflection about their writing. A reflection such as this can easily and effectively become part of a parent-teacher-student conference or a demonstration of learning. The reflection tool outlined at the top of page 44 was developed specifically for freewrites. However, it can be adapted to suit the needs of any genre or assignment.

As you prepare for a demonstration of learning or a parent-teacher-student conference, ask students to choose their favorite freewrite to take to a final stage. The students can then write a reflection for their parents:

```
┌─────────────────────────────────────────────────────────────┐
│                   Freewriting Reflection                      │
│                                                               │
│  This is an example of freewriting. My prompt was _____  │
│                                                               │
│  During freewriting we are supposed to _____  │
│                                                               │
│  _____   │
│                                                               │
│  I like this piece of writing because _____ │
│                                                               │
│  _____   │
│                                                               │
│  After meeting with my writing group, I changed, added,       │
│  deleted_____                                           │
│                                                               │
│  _____   │
│                                                               │
│  My current writing goal is _____  │
│                                                               │
│  _____   │
│                                                               │
└─────────────────────────────────────────────────────────────┘
```

This reflection requires students to acknowledge what they are good at and where they might need to focus more effort. Most important, they are also required to set specific goals to improve their writing. Often I conference with my students soon after they complete a reflection such as this, enabling us to talk further about what they want to improve upon. I then learn how I can assist them with meeting the goals they have set for themselves.

Ask your students to choose one recent piece of writing that you will assess. They will pick their favorite of the last four or five pieces of writing they have completed. Talk to the students about why you allow for this choice. How do they feel about being able to choose which piece of writing to hand in? Most students appreciate the opportunity to choose as there will be some pieces of writing that they like more than others. Assessing each piece of writing is overwhelming for both the students and the teacher. Letting students choose what to assess gives them more freedom on the day of initial writing as they know that what they write will not necessarily be assessed.

Choice of Freewrite for Assessment Made Easy

In my class, students use loose-leaf paper for their freewriting. They keep their freewrites in the Freewriting section of their language arts binders for ease of removal (students take the page out of their binders when they meet with their writing groups). They also staple the other students' feedback strips to the back of the appropriate freewrite page once they are complete. Drafts of the freewrites can go one behind the other.

I find this method of organizing freewrites much easier than using a duotang or even a scribbler. Duotangs make the taking in and out of the pages cumbersome. As for scribblers, they don't allow for future drafts to be kept with the first draft. If a student is choosing one of every four or five freewrites to take to a polished state, you won't want to leave a page in between for a revised draft. You won't know which freewrite students will later choose.

At the beginning of the Freewriting section of their binders, students insert a copy of a tracking sheet. Each day we write, they record their freewrite, creating a table of contents. I have found this practice useful whenever I have asked students to find the freewrite they wrote on a particular day or with a particular prompt.

I, too, keep track of our freewrites in this way. My comments on the tracking sheet are less about my own writing and more on what I notice about student writing on that day. For example, as indicated below, maybe Ayla and David had trouble keeping pen to paper; I would make note of that. Students learn to comment on the process for themselves, too.

A blank tracking sheet appears as a line master on page 48.

Freewriting Tracking Sheet			
Date Completed	**Topic/Prompt**	**Writing Time**	**Comments**
Sept. 6, 2016	I remember …	7 minutes	Ayla and David struggled to write the entire time.
Sept. 8, 2016	I feel …	8 minutes	Ayla wrote entire time; David slightly better.
Sept. 9, 2016	I'm worried about …	8 minutes	Sarah emotional during writing

Writing to Learn

"Writing to learn doesn't always mean producing finished, polished writing. Informal, scrappy, incomplete, poorly spelled writing can also serve as a means of coming to know." — Marion Crowhurst (1993, 19)

Once freewriting is established it works well in every subject area. When students write in response to a science lesson, a social studies video, or a debate about current events, they are engaging in a process of *writing to learn*. The process of freewriting helps students to formulate their thoughts about topics you are covering or experiences they are having.

Students often express their surprise at things they have written. By writing about their learning, they are forced to formulate their thoughts, to think about their thinking. Instead of just listening to a lesson or observing an experiment, students who write about their learning become more engaged and take more ownership in their learning. Instead of being passive learners, they become active. I remember clearly one student exclaiming, "I didn't know I thought that!" We had a good chuckle but then as a class, we discussed what she meant by her comment. To me, her exclamation sums up the idea of *writing to learn*.

Freewrites that are done in other subjects could be kept in the same spot as the language arts freewrites. When students are choosing a freewrite to bring to a more polished stage, they can also draw on their work from other subjects. The other option for organization is to have a separate scribbler or notebook for each subject where students will freewrite regularly. If this freewriting becomes a regular occurrence in other subject areas, students are truly going to experience writing to learn. Students begin to see how our learning is interconnected and not always neatly compartmentalized into subject areas.

An effective prompt in any subject is this: "Tell me what you know about this topic, and write one question that you have about this topic." Other prompts can be more specific to the subject area or topic.

Cross-Curricular Connection: Science

Freewriting in science class can be highly effective for students to construct meaning, make predictions, and solidify their understanding. In fact, in the Alberta Science curriculum, students are expected to "reflect and interpret" for all topics of study. Let's say your Grade 1 class is beginning a unit on seasonal changes. You could show your students pictures of the four seasons and ask them to write about what they notice. They could use the prompt "I see …" By having students write about what they see (students still unable to write independently could draw a picture as their response), they will begin to construct their own meaning before you even begin teaching the unit.

On another day, you could show pictures of various animals in hibernation during the winter (bears, frogs, and bats, for example). The writing prompt could be, "These pictures are the same because …" And even though you have chosen the pictures to show animals in hibernation, your students may not realize this. The writing that they are doing is not expected to reach the "right" conclusions. It is meant to be an avenue to learn, to observe, and to think deeply about a topic. Students might notice that the pictures all show animals who are sleeping; they might notice that there is snow in each of the pictures; they might notice that the animals all seem to be curled up. So, although they may not use the word *hibernation* in their writing, all of these observations are valuable as you teach this concept.

Any science topic can be approached this same way. For a class learning about wheels and levers, for example, I might bring in my Whirley Pop Popcorn Maker, a bicycle, and a clock and then ask students to write about any similarities they notice. After writing about it on their own, perhaps they could share with a partner and then add another few sentences to their writing. For a class learning about chemistry, I might explain the experiment we are about to conduct and then ask the class to spend four or five minutes writing their predictions and the reasoning behind these predictions. After the experiment, I would ask them to write again, this time about what they observed and how it might have differed from their predictions. As you can see, this writing is not about getting things "right." It is about writing to learn, putting the experiences and academic language into their own words, and making connections to what they are observing. Students will construct meaning through the writing they do.

Cross-Curricular Connection: Social Studies

In social studies, students are expected to think critically, respond to ideas and information, notice cause and effect, patterns, and trends, and make connections to their own lives. Writing to learn will assist students in developing all of these skills.

The social studies curriculum considers big ideas such as community, citizenship, and identity. Students can begin to form their own ideas and express their thoughts about these concepts through freewriting. In social studies, I often use questions to guide their writing. When formulating questions based on your current topic of study, be sure that the questions are open-ended to allow for a more thoughtful response. Some of these questions would be effective to use both at the beginning of a unit *and* at the end of the unit to show how student thinking and understanding have changed. If questions posed are too difficult, try more simple phrasing.

Simple phrasing allows the students to rewrite the prompt if they get stuck during the freewriting process and therefore encourages continuous writing. Sometimes with questions as prompts, students will simply stop writing. Decide what is best for your group of students.

- "What makes a community a community?" or "Community is …"
- "What traditions do you and your family celebrate?" or "My family traditions are …"
- "How is your life different from someone living in Iqaluit?" or "If I lived in Iqaluit …"
- "What responsibilities do you have as a member of your home?" "What responsibilities do you have as a member of society?" or "As a member of society, I am responsible for …"
- "How does the land in a region affect the society that lives there?" or "The land around our community …"

Too often, concepts such as these are only discussed and not written about. When we consider class discussions, as important as they are, they often involve only a small percentage of students in the talking and, therefore, the learning. By asking everyone to write and express their views, we can better engage all students in the learning process. Writing to learn becomes an important process for students, and they begin to look forward to the writing time especially knowing that it is not about assessment but about learning.

Cross-Curricular Connection: Art

With the teaching of elementary art, it is easy to focus on the act of creating art and less on reflecting on art itself or the process of creation. And yet, the Alberta curriculum, for example, focuses on four major components: reflection, depiction, composition, and expression. In the area of reflection, attention is given to three major aspects: analyzing structures in nature, assessing designed objects, and appreciating art.

Writing during art class may not seem necessary or natural for a lot of teachers, and yet I find that students particularly enjoy writing about art. Often, emotion is revealed through the writing, and students learn to respond to art in profound and meaningful ways. While looking at a Monet painting, students respond, "This painting makes me feel …" or "I like how …" With a collection of pictures, paintings, and photographs with mostly warm colors, they explore, "I notice …" or again, "I feel …" After looking at a collection of paintings about nature, they consider, "All of these paintings …" In examining photographs of a variety of flowers, they observe, "These flowers are the same [or different] because …" or simply, "I see …" After the experience of fingerpainting, students write, "Today when I was painting …"

The possibilities of freewriting are endless. As you become more familiar with the process, you will find infinite opportunities to use it within your classroom, and you will quickly see its benefits. Your students will *learn to write* more effectively and they will *also* be *writing to learn*.

Freewriting Tracking Sheet

Date Completed	Topic/Prompt	Writing Time	Comments

5
Journal Writing

"Journal writing is a voyage to the interior."
— Christina Baldwin

When rereading my own journal entries, I have often been surprised at my thinking. Journal writing is certainly *a voyage to the interior* and can uncover unexpected insights. Why not provide students with this opportunity?

Journal writing, besides providing more time to write, is an opportunity to form connections with our students and give them time for introspection. As teachers, we know that students are often eager to share stories and events from their own lives. Unfortunately, time does not always afford us the luxury of listening to every story our students yearn to tell us. Through journals, all students are given the opportunity to share their own experiences, feelings, and opinions with us.

My students know that their journals represent a private exchange between teacher and student. This understanding affects the intimacy of their topics and their freedom to explore their own thoughts, emotions, and ideas. So, when your students are writing in their journals, be sure to honor this privacy. Do not share their writing with other students or colleagues unless you have a serious concern for the well-being of the student or someone else based on what was written.

A Tool for Reflection and Coping

Remember that journal writing is about personal expression; there is no right or wrong way to write in a journal. Some students may *choose* to write in their journals in the form of songs or poetry.

The process of writing provides an opportunity for self-examination and reflection. Through writing, including journal writing, our students can develop their sense of self in the world during their formative years. Linda Laidlaw (1998) explains the power of writing as this: "Together, through our shared stories we might find our real lives" (131). Consider songwriting. Many musicians and songwriters have written songs after tragic or distressing life events. Eric Clapton wrote about the heartbreaking death of his four-year-old son in "Tears in Heaven." The act of writing, whether through song, poetry, journal entries, or memoir, can add permanence and significance to our emotions and experiences. Some poets and writers may not address their own struggles directly but, instead, explore events that have had an impact on their culture or society. "American Pie," composed by Don McLean, was written in response to the 1959 plane crash that killed Buddy Holly, Ritchie Valens, and The Big Bopper. Alan Jackson wrote the song "Where Were You (When the World Stopped Turning)" in response to the events of September 11, 2001: his song captures the raw and widespread emotions of the day. Although we do not often ask our students to write songs, journal writing provides the same opportunity to express one's emotions and thoughts.

"I write because I don't know what I think until I read what I say."
— Flannery O'Connor

Writing in a journal can become a coping mechanism for students going through difficult times. Universal emotions — love, loss, sadness, anger, confusion — can sometimes be difficult to cope with and process. Through writing, students can identify and acknowledge their emotions and begin to deal with them; perhaps they can even find hope and resolve as they put a voice to their feelings.

Journal writing is a form of writing used at all grade levels with great effectiveness; however, the approach in the various grade levels varies slightly.

Journal Writing in Kindergarten

Our Kindergarten students come to us with a range of exposure to language. Regardless, though, drawing is a child's first form of writing. Children are communicating through their pictures. Eventually, with instruction and exposure, they will begin to add writing to their journal entries. Initially, pictures suffice.

Kindergarten journal entries should be written on blank paper. Even if students begin to include strings of letters, they generally have not yet developed enough fine motor control to utilize lines on a page. Therefore, provide blank paper and get into the habit of date-stamping each entry to help track their progress.

I plan for my Kindergarten students to write journal entries two or three times each week. I create a personal portfolio for each student and then save one or two of their journal entries each month to show the progress of the students during a term or throughout the year. On some days, I send the journal entries home. Sometimes, I use their journal entries to create a class book that can be laminated and coiled for students to *read* throughout the year.

How do we initiate journal entries with these young students? I model ideas for them. For example, before we sit to write, we gather on the carpet and talk about what we might write about. I might say, "Last night, I went to a hockey game. I think I'll write about that today. What do you think *you* might write about?" Students of this age are rarely short of things to share! Once we have engaged in this talk time, we move to the tables and begin to *write*.

The temptation is to provide a prompt for our young writers each day they write. You can certainly provide options, but do not insist that students write on a specific topic. In my experience, Kindergarten students often begin drawing and sometimes they are not sure where they are headed. As they draw, the idea develops. You can see how prompts might be limiting for students of this age.

On occasion, I might ask all students to write on the same general topic. If we have recently gone on a field trip, I might ask students to write about their experience. Or, if we have recently read *Alexander and the Terrible, Horrible, No Good, Very Bad Day* by Judith Viorst, I might plan to have students write journal entries about their own terrible, horrible, no good, very bad days. These entries can then be put together as a class book. In such a context, I would ask students to write about the given topic. Otherwise, I keep it open-ended.

It can be helpful to model a journal entry on chart paper or on the Smartboard. I begin by talking about my topic, drawing a picture (and talking through what I'm adding), and writing a sentence. By my modelling, students may begin to include letters or mock letters on their page. (See Chapter 11 for more details.)

"Tell me about your writing."

In Kindergarten, keep your writing time to about 10 minutes. Typically, this is about as long as students of this age will be engaged. Slowly, lengthen the time as they are able. When students are nearing the end of their writing time for the day, be sure to say, "Tell me about your writing." Keep this statement open-ended to ensure that you do not mistake what they have drawn. There is nothing worse than asking Noah to talk about his dinosaur when he's drawn a dog!

If you have an educational assistant or parent volunteers in the room, train them to scribe student statements on the page (or on the back of the page). As much as possible, try to write what the students say. If something does not make sense, it is all right to rephrase it slightly, but stay as true as possible to the student's voice.

Notice that although Kindergarten students are primarily drawing pictures at the beginning, I use the word *writing*: What do you think *you* will *write* about? Tell me about your *writing*. Eventually, their journal entries will include both pictures and writing of some form.

Journal Writing in Grades 1 and 2

In Grades 1 and 2, my students write in journals several times each week. Beginning writers especially require time to talk about the topic before they start writing. As I do with the Kindergarten students, I gather my Grade 1 or 2 students on the carpet before our writing time. I give an example of what I could write about: "This weekend I was planting my garden. I think I'll write about that today. What do you think *you* will write about?" This talk time will help students generate ideas and vocabulary and make the writing process itself less intimidating. With very young writers I also use simple sentence prompts to help them generate ideas: I can …, I wish …, I like … The wonderful thing about these sentence starters is that students can write about anything. They are not bound by the topic of winter or a day at the beach. The prompts are open-ended.

Sometimes, I capitalize on current events in our classroom or school. For example, one day in Grade 2, after a student from another country became part of our class, we began talking about Canada. The conversation was energized and motivating for the students so I decided to carry on the topic in their journal writing. Their writing, too, proved to be full of energy. On that day our spontaneous conversation became the writing prompt.

Some young students may prefer to draw a picture *before* writing their sentences to help generate ideas. As a beginning teacher I was leery of this practice; in fact, I insisted that my students write first and draw the picture afterwards. I now understand that for some students, their drawing is their prewriting and helps them generate their ideas.

Students at the very beginning stage of writing might only draw and label a picture. Fortunately, writing allows for easy differentiation: allow choice in the process and change the expectation of quantity depending on the abilities of your individual students. Be wary of saying to the class, "Write a full page today." This direction may be unrealistic for some and too limiting for others. Make your guidelines individual. They don't have to be spoken each day. You will usually know when to ask a student to push a little further and when to accept what you have received.

Journal Writing for Grades 3 and Up

When I teach older students, I borrow an idea that my own Grade 7 language arts teacher used. We wrote each Monday morning in a journal he titled our "Weekend Update." The title was clever for those students whose typical response to a writing activity was "I don't have anything to write." Because it was a weekend *update* the students were instructed to write about their weekend: it gave everyone something to write about even if it became a chronology of events. Our teacher would write back to us each week.

A Therapeutic Process

For me, this journal became a coping mechanism that I looked forward to each week. At the time, my father had recently been diagnosed with multiple sclerosis. Within the pages of my scribbler, I was able to express the myriad of feelings that I was masking at home. I looked forward to the writing and I also looked forward to my teacher's response.

As with my own experience, a glance at history reveals this same phenomenon: when individuals are facing difficult circumstances — or after they have survived difficult circumstances — they write. Consider Anne Frank, Nelson Mandela, Viktor Frankl, and Solomon Northup. Journal writing is not about the end result, but the process, which is therapeutic. Without it we may be unaware of the situations our students are facing; through the writing of a journal, a student may find solace and hope.

Generating Topics

The most important thing to remember when students are writing in a journal is not what they are writing about but simply that they are writing. Therefore, provide options. There are many ways to provide journal topics for your students, including these:

- Write a question or statement on the board that the students *could* respond to during journal writing. "What is your favorite thing to do?" "What would you do if you were being bullied every day?" "Describe in detail the meals you ate over the Christmas holidays." "What is something you dislike about yourself?" "I feel happy when ..."
- Provide your students with a list of journal topics that they could glue into the front of their scribbler for easy reference.
- Give students a tic-tac-toe board filled with topics. During each journal writing time, they choose a square and color it in. Eventually, they will write about every topic on the tic-tac-toe board, but students are motivated because they have choice on each particular day.
- In the classroom, provide a journal jar from which students can choose a topic. Students could also add to the journal jar if they think of an appropriate topic (approved by you, of course).
- Create cubes with a topic listed on each side. Students roll a cube to choose their topic for the day.
- Create a spinner with various journal topics.

Although providing options is helpful, it is important to allow students to choose their own topic if they wish. A student in your class may be waiting eagerly for the opportunity to write about something specific just as I was when I was a student.

When I know that a student is struggling with something in life, I equip that student with a journal from my stash. This journal is separate from anything students are expected to complete in class; it is a gift I give to a student who might need an extra outlet. I never ask to see that journal again. I explain how writing has benefited me in times of turmoil or uncertainty and how I hope that it can do the same for my student.

Topic Ideas
Dreams, pets, sports, collections, grandparents, fears, worries, friends, songs, movies, food, candy, colors, places (the beach, the zoo, school, home, a friend's house), shoes, clothing, cell phones, haircuts, board games, walks, chairs, flowers, wood

A Caveat

Generally, I have found that once freewriting has been established, journal writing becomes more natural for students, as well; however, if we let them, some students would take the entire writing time choosing their topic. Set the expectation: within two or three minutes, students must be writing. Be proactive and provide many options. If you notice a student who chronically avoids this writing time, conference with that student to determine why he or she is avoiding the task.

Other Journal Writing Ideas

Periodically I give my students a specific writing task for their journal. Here are some of the tasks I have used.

- Without any other instruction, ask students to pick a favorite celebrity or sports figure. After they have chosen the individual, they are to write a journal or diary entry as if they were that person. They are to keep the identity a secret for others to guess. This is one of the rare occasions when I ask students to share their journal entries with a peer or with the class. Because they are writing from the point of view of someone else, I don't see the sharing as an infringement on their privacy. Students enjoy the guessing game component!
- Ask students to write a journal entry from the perspective of someone else in the family: a parent, a sibling, even the family pet. I would not ask students to share these entries with anyone.
- On one day, introduce this journal entry prompt: "The best thing about technology is …" Then, on the next day: "The worst thing about technology is …"
- Have the class build a journal entry as a shared writing activity. Choose a student to write down the entry as it is dictated either on the whiteboard or on a page of loose-leaf. The catch? Each person in the class can say only one word at a time. Go around the room until each student has contributed a couple of words. Read the entry out loud at the end. The result? Likely, one silly journal entry and a whole lot of laughs.

Special Journals: Math and Visual

As noted in Chapter 4, I often use freewriting in subjects such as social studies or science. Journals, too, can be used in other subject areas as a means of reflection. In addition to their regular journals, my students have a math journal and a visual journal. Math journals can be used by students to show their work, their thinking processes, and their evolving understanding of mathematical concepts. Visual journals are one of my favorite tools to help students reflect and respond creatively in all subject areas.

Cross-Curricular Connection: Math Journals

Math journals have become a more recent addition to many classrooms. As educators who understand more about the constructivist approach to learning, we tend to favor methods that help students construct meaning and reflect on their learning processes. Through math journals, teachers can gain much insight into a student's current understanding of the math concepts being taught.

Math journals can be used for reflection through questions or prompts given by the teacher. Reflection can occur before a unit, during a unit, or as a culminating activity. For example, before beginning a unit on division, students may be asked, "What do you already know about division?" As the unit progresses, the prompt might be, "What did you learn today?" or "What questions do you have about what we learned today?" or "In your own words, explain the meaning of _____." At the end of the unit, you could give the prompt "Tell me the two or three most important things you learned in this unit." At the end of a term, effective questions would be, "What are you proud of in math this term? What did you find challenging this term?" Notice that these prompts are open-ended and, therefore, allow for a wide range of responses.

Math journals typically move students into deeper thinking about their own learning and even the emotion that many students feel during math class. Prompts can be given to determine student attitudes about math: "I love math because ..." "Math is difficult when ..." "People who are good at math ..." Through reading these reflections in math journals teachers can be in tune with the attitudes, frustration levels, and moments of accomplishment of their students.

Another effective use of math journals is frequently asking for a connection to the real world. After a lesson on fractions or graphing, skip counting or multiples, students could write a reflection using this prompt: "I will use this skill when I ..." or "Connect _____ to real life."

Our current math curriculums involve frequent use of manipulatives. Math journals can be used to document the processes and learning that occur while students use manipulatives. Over the years, I have used the program *Box Cars and One Eyed Jacks* with my students. These games reinforce the skills and concepts I am teaching. A math journal can be an effective way to occasionally document the learning that occurs while playing dice or card games. The task for students after a dice game could be to illustrate all the different combinations that could be used to make 7. As well, they would have to write the accompanying number sentences ($0 + 7 = 7$, $1 + 6 = 7$, $2 + 5 = 7$, $3 + 4 = 7$).

As with journals in other subject areas, do not assess your students' journal writing in mathematics. The journals will provide you with information for report card comments and such, but your focus is on the content: students' understandings, strategies, and misconceptions. Be sure to allow students to use words, pictures, and symbols to explain their thinking. Ultimately, writing in math journals leads students to clarify their thinking by slowing down the process and understanding it more fully. It forces students to look more closely at the vocabulary used in math and to make connections to the real world.

Cross-Curricular Connection: Visual Journals

Visual journals are an effective way of using words and pictures to provide an opportunity for students to encapsulate their learning. They are typically used in multiple subjects, allowing students to, for example, illustrate the steps of a science experiment, include a graphic organizer comparing life in their own community and life in another region of study, or illustrate the beginning, middle, and end of a text read. The possibilities are endless.

One of my favorite uses of visual journals is as a response to literature. After reading something aloud to your students (the end of a novel, for instance), ask students to respond visually to the text. This is a curricular outcome, one that taps into our students' creative minds. It can be revealing to see what they create.

I give them an extended time for this and ask that it be done without conversation. I usually put on some music and give the students about half an hour. The first few times my students complete this task, we review the types of responses they could make (see Chapter 9 for more details). They may include a connection to their own lives. They may use both pictures and words. They can choose from a variety of mediums: magazines, collage, pencil crayons, ink, and so on.

Another excellent use of visual journals is to have students represent a particular word, phrase, or quotation. The same word might be given to all students to illustrate if it's connected to something the class has been discussing. The word could be quite abstract, perhaps *hope*, *joy*, *balance*, *love*, or *peace*, or it could be slightly more literal, as in *home*, *hero*, or *family*. You could also ask students to come up with a one-word response to a lesson you taught and then illustrate the word of their choosing.

Quotations can also generate revealing and thoughtful illustrations and responses. Students record the quotation and the name of the author on the page and then illustrate and reflect around it. Try these:

- "Life is a gift." — Tony Robbins
- "Be yourself. Everyone else is taken." — Oscar Wilde
- "You're braver than you believe, stronger than you seem, and smarter than you think." — A. A. Milne, *Winnie-the-Pooh*
- "Fall seven times, stand up eight." — Japanese proverb
- "Mistakes are proof that you are trying." — Author unknown
- "No act of kindness, no matter how small, is ever wasted." — Aesop, "The Lion and the Mouse"
- "We shall never know all the good that a simple smile can do." — Mother Teresa
- "My best friend is the one who brings out the best in me." — Henry Ford
- "I like nonsense. It wakes up the brain cells." — Dr. Seuss
- "I am not afraid of storms, for I am learning how to sail my ship." — Louisa May Alcott, *Little Women*
- "A dog owns nothing, yet is seldom dissatisfied." — Irish proverb
- "If you can't feed a hundred people, then just feed one." — Mother Teresa
- "It has been a terrible, horrible, no good, very bad day. My mom says some days are like that." — Judith Viorst, *Alexander and the Terrible, Horrible, No Good, Very Bad Day*
- "You have brains in your head. You have feet in your shoes. You can steer yourself any direction you choose." — Dr. Seuss, *Oh, the Places You'll Go!*
- "A book is a gift you can open again and again." — Garrison Keillor
- "Adventure is worthwhile in itself." — Amelia Earhart
- "Somewhere the hurting must stop." — Terry Fox
- "You were made to be awesome." — "Kid President" Robby Novak
- "Even the darkest night will end and the sun will rise." — Victor Hugo

Once visual journals are set up, they are useful on those inevitable days you are planning for a sub. They are also good for your fast finishers: students can return to finish or add to previous entries. Be sure that students get into the habit of putting a date on their work. Over time, visual journals provide fascinating insight into the artists behind them.

A visual journal is also effective either during or after a field trip. The request could be quite simple: "Respond to your learning today" or "Capture your day on the page." As much as possible, we complete the visual journal entry on the

A good idea is to start a collection of your favorite quotations to inspire visual journal entries. Invite your students to share their favorites too!

day of the field trip or the following day. It loses some of its power as we distance ourselves from the experience.

My students begin their week with a written journal entry; they end their week with half an hour in their visual journals. Sometimes the prompt is open-ended: "Show me what you learned this week" or "Illustrate the *best* part of your week." Other times the prompt is quite directed: "Illustrate how you used your five senses this week" or "Draw the weather to indicate your mood." As students gain more experience with visual journals, their entries tend to become more profound and meaningful. Visual journals provide students with time to reflect, reconnect, and tap into their thoughts and emotions.

Visuals journals provide a wonderful opportunity for gallery walks. To engage in this type of sharing, students walk quietly around the class looking at the journal work of their peers. Gallery walks often encourage students to do their best work because they know that others will be seeing what they have done. They also allow students to see the wide variety of responses possible. Another student's work might inspire a future entry. The idea of a community of learners obviously comes into play to ensure that students respect each other's work.

The Status of Assessment

Whatever the grade level we teach, we give value to our students' writing by providing written responses, even with just a sentence or two. Our comments work best as conversational remarks about the content that serve to help us connect with our students and value them as individuals. Asking questions within responses could elicit the next entry. For example: "Jordan, I can see you love playing hockey! Tell me about this. How long have you played? What is the name of your team?" Teacher responses should not focus on correcting the writing.

Allow student journals to be a place of expression without assessment being a factor. Journal entries should never be assessed.

By providing our students with opportunities to journal, we give them a way to connect to us as teachers and a means to engage in helpful introspection and reflection.

If a day's entry is too personal, the student can simply close his or her book on that day.

Your students will look forward to your responses: a motivating reason for them to read!

6

Narrative Writing

"Stories make us more alive, more human, more courageous, more loving."
— Madeleine L'Engle

Over the course of her career, Madeleine L'Engle wrote more than 60 books. Perhaps she is best known as the author of *A Wrinkle in Time*, which won the John Newbery Medal and is often referred to as a classic for children.

What Madeleine L'Engle writes is true of the stories we read, but for many, the thought of *writing* stories brings a different perspective to the matter. Imagine this scene: the teachers from your school sit in a staff meeting. The principal says: "Okay, we have one last thing on the agenda. In the next hour, before you leave here today, each of you is going to write a narrative story." I would expect that most staff members at most schools would react in horror. Most would be flustered, anxious, overwhelmed, fearful even. Some might laugh out loud!

Given the reaction of most adults to being asked to write a narrative story, we can assume that many students are daunted by the task as well, especially as they get older. The way we approach this form of writing will have an impact on both our students' attitude towards the process and their learning of the skills.

Learning from Literature

Writing a narrative story is a skill very different from journal writing or freewriting. Why do we want students to do it? This form of writing fosters our students' creativity and stirs their imaginations. The focus in narrative writing shifts from our own lives into the lives of the characters we create. Students learn to develop different skills than they would from other forms of writing: the creation of plot, narrative structure, dialogue, character development, and setting. It is not that we want (or expect) all of our students to become authors, but through the process of narrative writing, students can practise and refine their own writing skills and ultimately learn to appreciate the artistry in the texts they read.

I find an excuse at every turn to read a picture book to my class no matter the age — literature offers such enriching experiences. In addition to serving as excellent models for our writing, literature can help us make connections, learn from the mistakes of others, gain empathy and compassion, acquire knowledge, and ultimately, define ourselves. We are able to time-travel to ancient Rome, we may be stranded on a deserted island, or we may find ourselves living in a world without color. Literature is a powerful teaching tool: instead of telling students that discrimination based on race is wrong, we can *show* them, using the experiences of others through story. The author creates memorable characters and through our imaginations we can explore and evaluate circumstances to determine our values and beliefs.

Through literature, we can try on different hats and experiment with various roles through the characters we encounter. For example, at about the same time, I read *The Art of Racing in the Rain*, a narrative told from the point of view of a dog, and *Room*, told from the point of view of a five-year-old. Both books stayed with me long after I closed their covers. Consciously or unconsciously, we are changed by the words we read: our exposure to the ideas, experiences, and thoughts of others can uncover, shape, confirm, and sometimes even alter who we are as individuals. "Emotional stirrings help to bind kids to reading in a splendid relationship that creates literacy" (Fox 1993, 141).

Read, Read, and Read Out Loud Some More

Read, read, and read some more to your students — no matter their age. Many years ago, when I was a student in Grade 12, my English teacher wept as she sat on top of an empty student desk, reading *King Lear* to us, the book spread open across her lap. She most certainly loves literature. Whether it be *Chicka Chicka Boom Boom* to our Kindergarten students or *The Giver* to our Grade 6 students, read out loud. Not only does this allow us to share our favorites, but it also provides students with an opportunity to hear both effective reading *and* effective writing. By listening to the work of good writers, we increase our vocabulary, intuitively learn rhythm, internalize the structures of language, and make meaning from text.

Teaching the Components over Time

As evident from my sample year plans in Chapter 2, I teach narrative writing throughout the school year, not during one brief unit only. There is too much to cover to teach it effectively in a short time, and narrative writing is a complex process that involves many components. Therefore, we should view the teaching of narrative writing as something we build on from month to month, having many literary conversations along the way. During the process, students become incredibly familiar with the rubric used for narrative writing. When students write narratives throughout the year, there is plenty of time to meet with writing groups, explore the various elements of narrative writing, and use the rubric to self-assess their own work.

Three Teaching Insights
1. Using picture books as exemplars
2. Allowing variable amounts of time for writing
3. Introducing plot patterns

At the beginning of my career, I wasn't sure how to teach narrative writing effectively. In fact, my instructions would be quite simple: "Okay, class. It's time to write a story." Initially, I wasn't sure how to guide students in this genre.

As with my instinct in other areas, I began to use picture books as exemplars and then teach corresponding mini-lessons. I noticed improvement. My students' narrative writing improved even further when I no longer required them all to write a story in the same amount of time. In retrospect, how unrealistic to assume that all 25 students could begin and end a story in the same time frame! My third breakthrough came when I began to teach plot patterns to my students. Many years ago, I attended an in-service given by JoAnne Moore who first introduced me to the idea of plot patterns.

Plot Patterns

After the in-service and the more I used literature to guide my teaching, the more I noticed patterns in the stories we read: for example, the ones I found resurfacing were transformation stories, stuck stories, circle stories, competition stories, and quest stories. Although these are the plot patterns I have used with my students, you and your students may discover others. As students are taught to identify plot patterns in the books and stories they read, they tend to feel more confident in organizing and writing their own narratives.

There is rarely time in the year to cover all plot patterns, and there is no need. The purpose of introducing plot patterns is to give students something to grasp onto so they can more effectively plan and organize stories of their own. I introduce plot patterns one at a time, using several appropriate mentor texts for each. Even for the older grades, the use of picture books is most effective because they are relatively short. I begin with transformation stories because they tend to be the easiest for students to understand, and the mentor texts for this plot pattern are most appropriate just before Christmas. I find that stuck stories are also fairly easy for students to grasp and, therefore, teach that pattern next. When I decide on a third plot pattern to teach, I consider the grade level and my particular group of students.

How to Teach a Plot Pattern

My method of teaching a plot pattern is quite systematic. First, I read aloud one of the mentor texts. Next, I read a second example of the plot pattern we are studying and ask students if they noticed any similarities between the two books. After this discussion, I introduce the plot pattern and the graphic organizer to the students, referring to the mentor texts throughout. Then, I give the students a copy of the graphic organizer that they complete on their own or in partners. I allow them to choose either of the mentor texts we have read together to fill out the information.

Eventually, the same day or the next, I give my students the same graphic organizer and ask them to generate a story of their own using this plot pattern. I find it most effective to double-side the graphic organizer so the page is the same on both sides. On one side, students record the information about one of the mentor texts. They note the title and the author and then fill out the details about the story. On the other side, they begin to generate a story of their own. I tell them to write their own name where the organizer asks for the author. I do not expect them to write a title yet as this is often the last thing we do as authors of a story.

After their graphic organizer is complete, students meet with their writing groups to discuss their plans and receive feedback. It is only then that students begin to write their stories. As you can see, using a plot pattern naturally creates a narrative structure for the students. The notion of beginning, middle, and end becomes inherent in the planning for students of all ages.

Although this lesson can be a long one, I often find that students are excited and engaged so I let them begin generating their story on the same day the plot pattern is introduced. With some classes, I prefer to introduce the plot pattern and complete the first graphic organizer on the first day and then on a subsequent day, have students begin to plan their own stories and meet with their writing groups. Judge your group of students. You know your students best!

When your Grade 1 students (or older students with limited written language) are completing the graphic organizers, be open to a combination of words and pictures. The purpose of the graphic organizer is to help them plan and formulate their ideas: this can certainly be done through pictures, if necessary.

An Alternative to Using a Plot Pattern

Rewriting a familiar story like "The Three Little Pigs" also provides students with scaffolding in their narrative writing. You could challenge the students to write the story from a different character's point of view. Jon Scieszka's *The True Story of the Three Little Pigs*, which is told from the perspective of the wolf, is an excellent example of this approach.

1. Transformation Stories

In a transformation story, a character undergoes a change after a transforming event. I typically begin teaching how to write this kind of story in November. *How the Grinch Stole Christmas* by Dr. Seuss and *A Christmas Carol* by Charles Dickens are wonderful examples of transformation stories with obvious examples of characters that undergo dramatic transformations. The most important elements to focus on within a transformation story are *character development* and *the transforming event*.

For a line-master version of the graphic organizer, see page 77.

I begin by reading *How the Grinch Stole Christmas*. Before I do so, however, I ask students to pay close attention to the character of the Grinch because we will be talking about him when the story is finished. After I read the book to them, I ask students to describe the Grinch at the beginning of the story. Students have no difficulty generating ideas: greedy, grumpy, selfish, cruel, mean, and nasty quickly surface. Then, I ask my students to describe the Grinch at the end of the story: kind, generous, sorry, remorseful, and thoughtful.

Next, I write the word *transformation* on the board and underline the root word, *transform*. I ask the students if they have heard this word before. Without fail, someone eventually brings up the toy: Transformers. We discuss the toy and how it changes, or transforms, from one thing to another. This conversation establishes the foundation for students' understanding of transformation stories. Even my Grade 1 students grasp the meaning quite easily.

After we understand that the word *transform* means to change, we discuss why the Grinch changes from being grumpy and greedy to generous and kind. The *why* becomes what we call the "transforming event."

For other options, consider *The Very Hungry Caterpillar* which is a literal example of a transformation story and helps our younger students to grasp the concept. I also use *A Christmas Carol* by Charles Dickens with students of all grade levels. There are some excellent picture book versions of this classic; however, even if you don't have a copy, most students are familiar enough with the story that you can still discuss the character and transforming event.

Either in the same lesson or on a subsequent day, we read a second transformation story. I typically follow *How the Grinch Stole Christmas* with *The Invisible Boy*, written by Trudy Ludwig and illustrated by Patrice Barton. However, any of the books suggested (see page 61) would work. In *The Invisible Boy*, the main character transforms from being lonely and sad to accepted and happy. The illustrations also complement the conversation about transformation as Barton chose to draw the boy as black and white at the beginning of the story and eventually, after his transformation, he is drawn with color. Another reason I like using this text is because it deals with different characteristics than the Grinch and Scrooge; instead of transforming from greedy to generous, the character goes from being isolated to accepted.

After a second exposure to a transformation story, we discuss how the transforming event must be quite significant in order for the reader to believe that the character would make a change. "Would it be believable if we turned the page and the character is suddenly different? Of course not! Something has to happen to make this change occur and to make it believable to us as the readers." We look back to our two mentor texts to reinforce the importance of the transforming event. I show the students the graphic organizer which we talk through together. Then, by this point students are ready to complete the graphic organizer independently or in partners on either of the transformation stories we have read.

Once you have taught transformation stories to your students, they will notice them everywhere: other books you read and very often in movies. Transformation stories are quite common and I encourage students to let me know when they discover a new one.

After we have explored these sample transformation stories and completed a graphic organizer on one of them, I ask students to begin planning their own transformation story. Students use the graphic organizer once again, this time planning their own ideas. Once they have a plan in place, students meet in their writing groups to talk about their ideas. The time in the writing groups during the planning stage accomplishes several things: students have to articulate their plan and, therefore, it tends to be more thought out, and their writing group provides feedback about the character and the transforming event. Often, after students meet in their writing groups, I see them modifying or adding to their graphic organizer. This is all an-important part of the writing process. Now the writing can begin!

The Three-Page Approach to Writing a Transformation Story

If you teach Grade 1 or 2, consider giving your students three sheets of paper to help guide their transformation stories. My preference is blank on the top half of the page and interlined on the bottom. I number these pages for the students. I give them one page at a time, guiding them each step of the way.

For the first page, I instruct them to draw their character at the beginning of their story. I remind them to think about how the character is feeling or what he is doing at the beginning. After they have drawn their pictures, I ask them to begin their stories on this page by telling me about their character. I refer to the mentor text throughout, saying, for example: "Remember the beginning of *How the Grinch Stole Christmas*? The Grinch was unhappy and greedy. He was stealing toys and trees. This is what Dr. Seuss drew at the beginning of the story."

As they finish that page, I give them the second. Again, I instruct them to draw their pictures first. What do they draw? I ask them, "What happens in your story that makes your character want to change? Remember when the Grinch was standing ice-cold in the snow? He was puzzling and puzzling till his puzzler was sore. Every Who down in Who-ville was still singing without any presents at all! *This* was what made the Grinch change. What is going to make *your* character change?" After the picture is drawn I prompt them to continue their story by writing about this transforming event.

Finally, as students are ready for the third page, I guide them to think about what their character will look like and feel like at the end of their stories. This is often the easiest for students to draw. After drawing, they write the end of their stories.

This format tends to work well for Grade 1 students especially because I teach transformation stories relatively early in the year for Grade 1. For them to write the entire story at once and on their own would be quite challenging, but by dividing it into three pages, all students can find success. Consider this three-page format for students in upper grades who might need more scaffolding.

Effective Mentor Texts	Transformation Stories
Grades 1 to 6	*Bad Kitty* by Nick Bruel *A Christmas Carol* by Charles Dickens *The Crippled Lamb* by Max Lucado *How the Grinch Stole Christmas* by Dr. Seuss *The Invisible Boy* by Trudy Ludwig *The Monsters' Monster* by Patrick McDonnell *Raven Brings the Light* by Roy Henry Vickers and Robert Budd *The Ugly Duckling* by Hans Christian Andersen *The Very Hungry Caterpillar* by Eric Carle

2. Stuck Stories

In a stuck story, something or someone gets stuck. For some students, this simple idea provides the structure they need to include an effective beginning, middle, and end. I have found the mentor texts for stuck stories effective for students of all ages. No matter what grade I am teaching, I introduce the idea of a stuck story by reading several books to the students: *The Mitten* by Jan Brett, *Andrew's Loose Tooth* by Robert Munsch, and *Bug in a Vacuum* by Mélanie Watt. After reading two or three of these books (or others from the list below), I ask the students what the stories have in common. I tell them that these stories represent another plot pattern and ask them to figure out what it might be. It is motivating and empowering for them to come up with the answer and they always do!

After they figure out the pattern, the students and I work together to complete the graphic organizer for *Andrew's Loose Tooth*. Since I developed the graphic organizer to help students plan their own stories, I then ask them to use a copy of it to plan their own stuck story. Students need to come up with three ways that the characters try to get the object unstuck before the final method is successful. This requirement naturally encourages a more complete story.

After reading a few stuck stories, students are excited about planning their own. I motivate the students further by bringing out a tray full of objects as inspiration: a piece of fruit, a key, a ball cap, a coin, a playing card, a magnifying glass, and a piece of jewellery, for example. Students decide if or how one of these objects will feature in their stories.

Although the other books listed below are effective examples of stuck stories, the graphic organizer works best for *Andrew's Loose Tooth*. For a line-master version of it, see page 78.

Effective Mentor Texts	Stuck Stories
Grades 1 to 6	*Andrew's Loose Tooth* by Robert Munsch *Bug in a Vacuum* by Mélanie Watt *The Hat* by Jan Brett *The Mitten* by Jan Brett *Mrs. Toggle's Beautiful Blue Shoe* by Robin Pulver *Mrs. Toggle's Zipper* by Robin Pulver *Stuck* by Oliver Jeffers

3. Circle Stories

As another common plot pattern in literature, circle stories begin and end in the same place, physically or metaphorically.

The focus of my teaching for circle stories is repetition, as in *Are You My Mother?* by P. D. Eastman. There, a little bird hatches from his egg in his nest and his mother is nowhere to be seen. The baby bird goes out to look for her and encounters a kitten, a hen, a dog, a cow, a car, a boat, a plane, and eventually a "snort." The baby bird asks each of these if he or she is his mother. Eventually the "snort" picks up the baby bird and places him back in his nest. The baby bird's mother returns to the nest, too — the story has come full circle. Although *Are You My Mother?* is a book for younger students, it is a good example to use with students of all ages. For this plot pattern, I would begin with this book and complete the graphic organizer together before reading another example of a circle story.

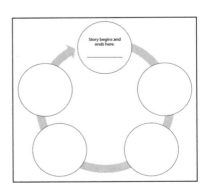

A line-master version of the graphic organizer appears as page 79.

Don't be afraid to read your Grade 6 students a picture book such as this. It will help solidify their understanding of the plot pattern, and secretly, they will probably enjoy the story.

Because this plot pattern varies so much, I tend to teach it after students have experience with at least two other plot patterns. It is easier for them to grasp it once they are quite familiar with the concept of a plot pattern.

In the graphic organizer, the top portion of the circle represents the beginning *and* the end of the story. For this book, I would have students write "the nest" in the top box; then, together, we would walk through the story remembering who the baby bird encountered and writing one label per box. When you work with your students, show them how to add more boxes as needed.

Once they have completed the graphic organizer for *Are You My Mother?* read several other examples and discuss how they would fit into the graphic organizer. Ask, "What makes this story a circle story?" Students will begin to notice that circle stories vary quite substantially.

The Little House and *Beyond the Pond* provide two examples. In *The Little House* by Virginia Lee Burton, a little house sits on a hill in the country. Over time, the little house watches the changes around her: roads and houses being built. Schools, stores, tall buildings, and a subway crowd her and she becomes unsettled. She misses the view of the sun and moon and stars. Eventually, the little house is moved out of the city to a perfect spot reminiscent of her first setting. She is back on a hill in the country, and the story has come full circle. In *Beyond the Pond*, Ernest D. and his dog decide to explore the pond in Ernest's backyard. This is where the story begins and ends. Ernest D.'s adventure in the pond changes him forever. Never again does he see the pond in quite the same way.

When they are planning their own circle stories, be open to your students' creativity. Emphasize that the story begins and ends in the same place — what happens in between is up to them!

Effective Mentor Texts	Circle Stories
Grades 1 to 6	*Are You My Mother?* by P. D. Eastman *The Best Nest* by P. D. Eastman *Beyond the Pond* by Joseph Kuefler *If You Give a Mouse a Cookie* by Laura Numeroff *Little Blue Chair* by Cary Fagan *The Little House* by Virginia Lee Burton *Too Much Noise* by Ann McGovern

4. Competition Stories

Key Questions to Address
• Who is competing?
• What kind of competition is it?
• What are they competing for?
• Who wins? How?

A line-master version of a graphic organizer appears as page 80.

In competition stories, two characters or groups compete against one another for some purpose. This particular plot pattern often begins with two characters, one bragging to the other. Then, a competition ensues. Aesop's "The Tortoise and the Hare" and "The Wind and the Sun" are the most effective to illustrate this plot pattern for students of all ages. Typically, one of the characters learns a lesson in a competition story. Although there are fewer mentor texts for this plot pattern, it is a pattern that students can relate to and enjoy writing.

Competitions come in many forms. When teaching this plot pattern, you may find it effective to brainstorm various types of competitions: singing, swimming, running, writing, public speaking, dance, tae kwon do, gymnastics, board games, card games, chess, and so on. I often encourage my students to pick something that they enjoy and may be involved in outside of school and use that as the basis for the competition within their story. That way, they already have some background knowledge that they can use as details within the story. This often helps with the creation of the setting and even the development of the characters.

Another helpful piece of advice for students writing competition stories is to have them create two quite different characters. The example of the Tortoise and the Hare becomes a good reference again here. The characters are very different physically and also in attitude. By asking students to imagine two very different characters, the problem within their story is often easier to plan and carry out. After the students create their story plan, I ask students to make character webs for each of their two main characters. Competition stories tend to follow a logical sequence of events and are therefore fairly easy for students to use as models.

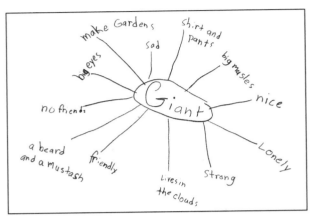

This Grade 2 student created her first character web about a giant. Her second character web will be for a character with different or even opposing traits. These two differing characters will set the stage for an effective competition story.

Effective Mentor Texts	Competition Stories
Grades 1 to 6	"The Tortoise and the Hare" by Aesop "The Wind and the Sun" by Aesop

5. Quest Stories

In quest stories, the main character is seeking something he or she desires, and some sort of journey is usually involved. Many students enjoy reading and writing stories of this type. Fantasy is a popular genre these days, and many of the stories within this genre fall into the category of a quest story. There is a wide range of quest stories and they are fairly simple for students to grasp. Quest stories are especially effective for upper elementary students because you can encourage them to include more elements in their stories.

My favorite mentor text to introduce the concept of quest stories to students is *The Wizard of Oz* by L. Frank Baum. I love the reaction when students realize that the original story was first published in 1900. I use a picture book version published by Random House and illustrated by Charles Santore. This story is the perfect introduction to quest stories and sparks much discussion about the elements of an interesting quest story. Although this book has been condensed from L. Frank Baum's original novel, it is still considerably longer than a traditional picture book. I plan to read it over the course of a week-and-a-half to two weeks.

I teach quest stories after other plot patterns. Therefore, students are familiar with the concept of the graphic organizer that accompanies the plot pattern. In this situation, I provide my students with the graphic organizer before we begin reading *The Wizard of Oz*. We discuss the elements of the quest story and then I ask them to look for these elements as I read the book out loud. In this case, we complete the graphic organizer over a period of days rather than all in one lesson.

A graphic organizer for quest stories should raise these questions:

• Who is on a quest?
• What are they searching for?
• What does the main character do to find what he/she is looking for?
• What obstacles does the character face?
• How does the character reach the goal?

A line-master version of a graphic organizer appears as page 81.

When motivating your students to write quest stories, keep in mind that the most important element to focus on is the *desired goal*. Discuss how the desired goal could be a physical object such as gold, a kind of treasure, or even a missing family locket. Talk, too, about the possibility of something less tangible, such as happiness, true love, a purpose in life, or even a way home as with Dorothy in *The Wizard of Oz*.

The other important element to focus on with your students are the *obstacles* the character will face during the quest. These obstacles in the way of reaching the desired goal are what make the story interesting and the successful quest more satisfying.

Be sure to provide several opportunities for students to meet in their writing groups while working on their quest stories. The feedback they get from their group will enhance their work.

Effective Mentor Texts	Quest Stories
Grades 1 to 6	*How to Catch a Star* by Oliver Jeffers *Miss Rumphius* by Barbara Cooney *The Paper Bag Princess* by Robert Munsch *The Wonderful Wizard of Oz* by L. Frank Baum (illustrated by Charles Santore)
Grades 5 to 6	*Harry Potter and the Deathly Hallows* by J. K. Rowling *The Hobbit* by J. R. R. Tolkien

It didn't take long to see how using plot patterns empowered my students to create more detailed, coherent stories. Now I cannot imagine teaching narratives any other way. In addition to teaching this concept, I also focus on four other important elements of narrative stories: (1) narrative structure, (2) dialogue, (3) character development, and (4) setting.

Narrative Structure: Beginning, Middle, and End

For students in junior high school or high school, we teach a fairly complex version of narrative structure with a focus on rising action, the climax, and falling action which ultimately leads to a resolution. In elementary school, I tend to focus on narrative structure more simply by using the terminology of *beginning*, *middle*, and *end*.

Teaching students about plot patterns will help to ensure that they include a beginning, middle, and end in their stories. The plot patterns have an inherent structure that students follow, but creating a full narrative structure still requires practice. To help students develop strong story plots that include a beginning, a middle, and an end, I have them plan and tell stories orally.

Using Wordless Picture Books

I begin by showing them a wordless picture book. First, we go through the pages as a class observing the pictures without saying anything. The second time through, I model the telling of the story on each page. Of course, my oral story is my interpretation of the pictures. An interesting option is to have a student use the same book to tell a different version of the story. Students can then be given wordless books and work in partners to practise telling oral stories.

These wordless picture books have another purpose in my classroom: I often choose one picture from a wordless picture book as a picture prompt to inspire student stories. In fact, in Alberta, Grade 6 students are required to write a story each spring based on a picture prompt provided on the *Provincial Achievement Test*.

<table>
<tr><th>Effective Mentor Texts</th><th>Wordless (or Almost Wordless) Picture Books for Teaching Narrative Structure</th></tr>
<tr><td>Grades 1 to 6</td><td>

A Ball for Daisy by Chris Raschka
Chalk by Bill Thomson
Float by Daniel Miyares
Fossil by Bill Thomson
Free Fall by David Wiesner
Journey by Aaron Becker
Lights Out by Arthur Geisert
The Lion and the Mouse by Jerry Pinkney
The Red Book by Barbara Lehman
Robot Dreams by Sara Varon
Rosie's Walk by Pat Hutchins
The Snowman by Raymond Briggs
Sidewalk Flowers by JonArno Larson
Spot, the Cat by Henry Cole
The Tortoise and the Hare by Jerry Pinkney
The Typewriter by Bill Thomson
Tuesday by David Wiesner
The Umbrella by Dieter Schubert
Wave by Susy Lee
Where's Walrus? by Stephen Savage
Zoom by Istvan Banyai

</td></tr>
<tr><td>Grades 3 to 6</td><td>

Bluebird by Bob Staake
One Scary Night by Antoine Guilloppe
Unspoken: A Story from the Underground Railroad by Henry Cole

</td></tr>
</table>

Showing Pictures with Possibilities

Effective prompts can be found by browsing your bookshelf or making a quick Internet search. When choosing picture prompts, I look for pictures with multiple possibilities and some sort of mystery or question. My favorite prompts come from the wordless picture books by illustrators such as Bill Thomson and David Wiesner. For this purpose, it is more effective if the students do not see the whole book before you complete this lesson.

I begin by showing students one picture that we then discuss together. We simply describe what we see in the picture: the character, the setting, the weather, the details. We make some inferences. "I notice that is snowing and that the little boy is dressed in a heavy coat and scarf: it must be a cold, winter day." After we have described the picture in full, I ask the students to think about which plot pattern they might use with this story. Students then orally share which plot pattern they have chosen and briefly describe their beginning, middle, and end. I ask for a few ideas for this picture to show how varied our ideas can be all stemming from the same picture.

The wordless picture books listed for Grades 3 to 6 deal with more mature content and would not be appropriate for younger students.

If you haven't yet taught plot patterns, you could ask students to think just about a beginning, a middle, and an end.

After we practise this as a whole group, students are partnered up and given a picture prompt. (I have a set of laminated illustrations I use for this purpose.) They complete the same activity we did as a whole group. First, they describe their picture in detail to each other. Second, they talk through a plot pattern including a beginning, a middle, and an end. I give students only 5 to 10 minutes for this task and often provide a second picture for another round of practice.

With some students, I find it helpful for them to record their ideas. I use large laminated pages set up like the sample below, and students can then use dry-erase markers to write their beginning, middle, and end as they are planning. Be open to a combination of words and pictures on this page, especially for very young writers.

Beginning	Middle	End

These lessons help students to more fully develop their stories when it comes time to write. Their content and organization should both show improvement.

Dialogue

Dialogue is an essential element in narrative writing. It is, therefore, important for students to distinguish between the actual dialogue in a story and the dialogue tags. There are many ways to teach this. One is to have students underline all of the dialogue on a page of text. It is very revealing to see students complete this task. Typically, strong readers can do this easily; struggling readers often haven't figured out the difference. Once students do realize the difference, both their reading and their writing tend to improve.

Another effective activity is to ask the students to read only the dialogue of a book out loud. This reveals whether the students know the difference between the dialogue and the other writing. It also begins the discussion about the importance of balancing the amount of dialogue and description in our writing. A story told only with dialogue can be frustrating and confusing to read. A story told without any dialogue can be quite dull. A balance between the two is essential.

Using Wordless Picture Books

One of my favorite lessons when teaching students about dialogue is to provide them with a wordless picture book and have them create their own conversation. I typically give one book to each set of partners. Students sit knee to knee and take turns creating dialogue. They can do this orally.

Effective Mentor Texts	Wordless (or Almost Wordless) Picture Books for Teaching Dialogue
Grades 1 to 6	*Chalk* by Bill Thomson *Lights Out* by Arthur Geisert *The Lion and the Mouse* by Jerry Pinkney *Robot Dreams* by Sara Varon *Sidewalk Flowers* by JonArno Larson *The Snowman* by Raymond Briggs *Tuesday* by David Wiesner *The Typewriter* by Bill Thomson *Wave* by Susy Lee *Where's Walrus?* by Stephen Savage
Grades 4 to 6	*Bluebird* by Bob Staake

Writing dialogue is a skill you can have students practise without asking them to write an entire story. For example, students can write a conversation between two characters or two objects: the principal and a student, a baseball and a glove, or a fork and a spoon.

Exploring Dialogue in Picture Books

I use various mentor texts when teaching dialogue. As a class, we explore the various ways dialogue is approached in picture books. *The Bee Tree*, *The Dot*, and *Yertle the Turtle* are usually the picture books I begin with. They all have excellent examples of effective dialogue that reveal character traits as well as effective dialogue tags. Though these are books I typically use, a quick look through your bookshelf will reveal many effective examples.

I also read various other books to show how dialogue can be dealt with in other ways. For example, in *Don't Let the Pigeon Drive the Bus!* author Mo Willems chooses to use speech bubbles and no dialogue tags. In *Ask Me* by Bernard Waber, the entire story is a dialogue between father and daughter and yet again, no dialogue tags and quotation marks are used. By exploring these examples, students have a better grasp of dialogue and its purpose. Ultimately, they begin to be more deliberate in how they use dialogue in their own writing.

Effective Mentor Texts	Dialogue
Grades 1 to 6	*Ask Me* by Bernard Waber *The Bee Tree* by Patricia Polacco *Don't Let the Pigeon Drive the Bus!* by Mo Willems *The Dot* by Peter H. Reynolds *I Want My Hat Back* by Jon Klassen *One Cool Friend* by Toni Buzzeo *Something from Nothing* by Phoebe Gilman *Yertle the Turtle* by Dr. Seuss

Discovering Dialogue Tags

Once the students have written conversations, such as those based on wordless picture books, discuss how to write dialogue tags. Some tags can be quite simple

(*Carla said*). Other tags might be more descriptive (*Carla said, looking shyly at her new teacher*). By writing conversations such as these, students enjoy the assignment while practising a necessary skill in story writing.

It is also important to teach the placement of dialogue tags. I begin the lesson by asking where dialogue tags are used in a sentence. Usually students realize that they can be at the beginning, as in "*Tim groaned*, 'I don't want to go to school.'" They are also aware that tags can be at the end, as in "'You know you have to,' *replied his mom*." Sometimes, a student will notice that tags can be in the middle of a sentence, too, as in "'Okay, I'll go,' *he said, picking up his backpack*, 'but I'm not going to like it.'"

After showing them some examples of all three placements, I give each student three sticky notes and a book. Students then have to flag a dialogue tag at the beginning, middle, and end of a sentence. Once they have done so, I ask some of the students to read their examples out loud. This reveals how well they understand the difference.

After I know that they have understood the three placements, I ask them to return to one of their own stories and underline the dialogue tags there. They are then to consider two things: first, where the dialogue tags are located in the sentence; and second, the detail (or lack thereof) in their tags. Students can add to and revise their story to include more effective dialogue and dialogue tags.

Discussing Dialogue

After some writing and revising time, students will take this story to their writing groups. The focus of the discussion will be on dialogue tags and the dialogue itself. Provide prompts to ensure effective conversation.

- *For the writers:* "Share an example of where you used description within a dialogue tag." "Share an example of dialogue that best shows the voice of your character."
- *For the listeners:* "What did you learn about the character through the dialogue the writer shared?" "What suggestions do you have to improve the dialogue and dialogue tags?"

For written feedback, you could provide a feedback strip such as this:

Name of Writer: _____   Name of Listener: _____
Date: _____
When I listened to your dialogue, I noticed …
Have you considered ….

Character Development

An interesting character makes the writing of a story that much easier. In order to create effective characters, it helps to study them as a class. Ask students to list memorable characters. They may suggest some from books and some from movies: either is fine. Capitalize on your students' interests when choosing characters to discuss. The more engaged the students are, the more effective the lesson will be. Discuss what makes these characters memorable.

For most, the characters have depth. They are not purely good or strictly evil. Often, the most effective characters are those that we sympathize with but who also possess flaws. This is true even in the simplest forms. Consider David from David Shannon's series: titles include *No, David!*, which won the Caldecott Medal; *David Goes to School*; and *David Gets in Trouble*. This series is an effective example even for older students. The texts are short, but we have a good understanding of the character. He is charming and likeable but typically getting into mischief. Another effective example to study as a class is Alexander from *Alexander and the Terrible, Horrible, No Good, Very Bad Day* by Judith Viorst or Scaredy Squirrel, a character created by Mélanie Watt.

Comparing Characters

Characters within student writing tend to be quite flat. To help students understand how to make their characters well rounded and, therefore, more interesting, I suggest some comparisons. Find a typical version of "The Three Little Pigs." For comparison, use *The True Story of the Three Little Pigs* by Jon Scieszka. Read the first version to the students. Then, ask students to describe the characters and record the information. Typically, the character descriptions for a basic version of the text are quite simple. After this discussion, read *The True Story of the Three Little Pigs*. When students are asked to describe the characters in Jon Scieszka's version of the story, they realize how much more personality and depth the characters have: the description of the wolf, in particular, becomes much more detailed and interesting. The wolf tries to gain our sympathy as he explains that he is making a cake for his dear old granny's birthday and he also has a terrible cold. Instead, he comes across as a trickster or even a liar. These details provide a context for the events in this version of the story, increasing the depth of the character of *the big, bad wolf*. This example becomes one you can refer to time and again when you are asking students to develop their own characters.

Overturning Stereotypes

Possible stereotypical characters: a prince, a princess, a king, a queen, a librarian, a teacher, a monster, a giant, a ghost. Consider animals, too: a monkey, a mouse, a tiger, a turtle. Be sure to stay away from cultural stereotypes.

Students can also explore stereotypical characters with unexpected characteristics. We have all seen or heard about families who name their pit bull terrier "Fluffy" or their mastiff, "Tiny." These examples help our students to understand how authors sometimes create contrast by intentionally giving characters unexpected characteristics. In *The Paper Bag Princess*, for example, the title character seems undaunted when a dragon burns down her castle, destroys her clothes, and carries off her prince. This princess dons a paper bag and searches for the prince. She is not elegant or sophisticated as one might expect her to be. Instead, she is feisty and spirited — a stereotype turned on its head. In *The Monsters' Monster*, we have a preconceived notion about what the monster will be like. The author surprises us (and the other characters) by creating a monster that is uncharacteristically kind and polite. Students enjoy coming up with characters that mimic this idea of playing with the unexpected.

Making Simple Comics

Another way to help students create interesting characters is to capitalize on their love of comics. Ask your students to create two main characters, a superhero and a villain perhaps, or two best friends. They could illustrate and even label their drawing with details about the characters. On a later day, ask them to write and illustrate their own six-panel comic or storyboard using the two characters they have created. Eventually they could feature these characters within a narrative story using the comic or storyboard to guide them.

Making Character Webs

After discussing effective characters, ask students to choose one of their favorite characters from a book or movie and to create a character web with the following categories to guide them: physical attributes, family members, hobbies/interests, personality traits, fears, and favorites (e.g., book, food, toy, movie). This activity forces them to think about all aspects of a character and not strictly the physical traits.

On another day, show your students the picture of a person (not someone famous or anyone they might be familiar with). With the picture visible to the students (on the Smartboard ideally), students again create a character web. This time they are inventing the details themselves rather than relying on those in the text or movie. This is one step closer to creating their own characters.

As teachers, we may be tempted to ask students to write a full paragraph describing the character, but students would not find this helpful. Rarely is this how details are used within stories. In effective literature, description is spread throughout the story. So, when they are working on developing their characters, I ask my students to make a character web (on the computer or iPad in the form of a Popplet, or mind map, or on paper). Instead of writing a whole paragraph about the character, they can learn how to use the information from the character web within their writing. There are several ways to accomplish this: within dialogue tags, within the dialogue itself, within dialogue from other characters, and through the character's actions and reactions.

Revealing Character through Dialogue

Dialogue tags can effectively reveal details about a character. For example:

- *Her long brown hair covering her eyes, Amanda mumbled,* "It's Saturday, Mom. Don't make me get out of bed."
- "Let's go, Dad. I don't want to be late for practice," *said Tom, baseball glove in hand.*

In the first example, we are provided with a physical description of Amanda through the dialogue tag. In the second example, we learn about one of Tom's hobbies. This strategy is one that will dramatically improve your students' writing.

A character can also be revealed within his or her dialogue. Students should recognize that a grandmother would speak differently than a father with three young children, and a teenage girl differently than a doctor. I challenge students

Students sometimes tend to include too many characters in their stories. The more characters, the more confusing the story. Encourage them to limit the main characters to two, three at the most. They may include a few secondary characters if needed.

The scenario?
A fire alarm begins ringing in a doctor's office.
The characters?

- A grandmother
- A father with three young children in tow
- A teenage girl
- A doctor

How would they react?

to write dialogue for various characters given the following scenario: *a fire alarm begins ringing in a doctor's office*. Students are invited to read one sentence of dialogue out loud and their peers guess which character was speaking. This exercise challenges students to think about what someone might say and how the person would say it. Students enjoy this activity so much that we often put a variety of other characters in all sorts of interesting scenarios.

Characteristics can also be revealed in the dialogue of another character. For instance:

- *"Marco, why do you look so frazzled today? Your hair isn't combed, you're wearing mismatched socks, and your shirt is inside out!"*
- *"Cynthia, close that book. You've been reading all day. It's dinner time and your brother and sister are waiting for you!"*

In the first example, we get a physical description of Marco. In the second example, we learn that Cynthia loves to read and that she has two siblings. The writer hasn't *told* the reader; the reader has been *shown* — all in a few short sentences.

It is also important to point out to students that our characters' actions and reactions can reveal a lot about them. For example, in *Creepy Carrots!* Jasper Rabbit is afraid that he is being followed by the carrots that he loves to munch on. His fear motivates him to dig a moat and build a fence to surround the creepy carrots. In *The Dot* by Peter H. Reynolds, Vashti lacks confidence in her drawing ability. She refuses to draw anything until her teacher tells her to make a mark. In frustration Vashti takes a marker and makes a dot. After the teacher frames her work, Vashti is motivated to do better than her first effort and make more dots. Her dots become more creative and colorful and she ends up with a whole collection. At the beginning of the story, Vashti appears frustrated and discouraged. By the end of the story, Vashti is empowered. Peter H. Reynolds never uses any of these words to describe Vashti: we learn how she is feeling through her actions and words.

When students understand how to weave details about a character into their writing, when they learn how a character's actions can reveal qualities and emotion, their stories will seem more sophisticated and much less forced.

Effective Mentor Texts	Character Development
Grades 1 to 2	*Bad Kitty* by Nick Bruel *Chrysanthemum* by Kevin Henkes *David Goes to School* by David Shannon *No, David!* by David Shannon *The Paper Bag Princess* by Robert Munsch *Stand Tall, Molly Lou Melon* by Patty Lovell
Grades 1 to 6	*Alexander and the Terrible, Horrible, No Good, Very Bad Day* by Judith Viorst *Creepy Carrots!* by Aaron Reynolds *The Dot* by Peter H. Reynolds *The Emperor's New Clothes* by Hans Christian Andersen *Frederick* by Leo Lionni *The Monsters' Monster* by Patrick McDonnell *On the Shoulder of a Giant* by Neil Christopher *Scaredy Squirrel* by Mélanie Watt *The True Story of the Three Little Pigs* by Jon Scieszka

Grades 5 to 6	*Maniac McGee* by Jerry Spinelli *Stargirl* by Jerry Spinelli *Wonder* by R. J. Palacio

Setting

Students often have a limited understanding of setting. They tend to think of it strictly in the sense of place. However, *setting* also refers to the time period and conditions of the story. A castle on a hot, sunny day in the summer of 2016 is very different from a castle on a cold, stormy night in the winter of 1216. The location may be the same, but the time period and other conditions are also important.

Writing about Their Surroundings

Begin teaching setting by asking students to write descriptively about their current location. Prompt them to describe the sights, the details, the sounds, and the distractions. Complete this activity in the style of a freewrite. Give the students the option of making it a list.

After the freewrite, ask for a volunteer to read his or her writing aloud. Discuss the writing as a class. What details did this writer use? What senses? Did he use colors? What feelings were conveyed in the writing? Then, do the same with another volunteer's work. Compare and contrast the two pieces of writing. What was the same about them? What was different? Remind students that all comments must be respectful and constructive.

Later that day (or on a subsequent day), move to a different location (the gymnasium, the playground, or the library) and have students write again. Ask students to reflect on their writing and compare the two experiences. Each time you do this, students will learn to include more details: details they might not have considered the first time.

Responding to Photos, Picture Books, and Postcards

Another activity that assists students in creating an effective setting in their writing is to show a picture of an interesting place: a castle, a beach, a glacier. Ask students to describe the place with as much detail as they can conjure up: the sights, the smells, the sounds, the weather, the people passing by. If you ask students to bring a photo from home, they will likely have a memory associated with the photo. For some students having this reference makes the writing easier. Consider posting all the photos your students have contributed (as well as others) on a bulletin board to inspire the creation of various settings within your students' writing.

Notice that we are using freewriting for all of these lessons on setting. Doing this allows for short lessons, increases the amount of writing students complete, and ensures that the environment is non-threatening. As with our character development, we rarely want to include an entire paragraph describing the setting of a story. Demonstrate how these details should be woven into the narrative itself. After practising with setting, students can revisit a story they have written previously and determine how to work in details. Once again, students should be meeting in their writing groups to share and strengthen their work.

As always, I use picture books to enhance our discussion. With the younger students, we use the texts as a read-aloud and engage in a discussion about

Freewriting on Setting

I tried the list version of a freewrite myself: "… a backyard finally worthy to sit in, a large bumblebee searching for an entrance to our home, a chainsaw slicing wood in the distance, the smell of the blossoms on the tree outside our window, the red bird feeder I bought in St. John's (so glad I did), the patches of grass that didn't grow back after the winter, the perennials that have sprouted back to life and seem to grow several centimetres each day, the jet streams in the sky, the fluff floating through the air, the breeze blowing my pages as I write, my favorite pen in hand …"

As you can see, a few short minutes spent describing my surroundings captured the setting. There's nothing magical about it, nothing profound. And yet, it breaks the barrier and frees the writer.

setting. For the older students, after an initial read-aloud, I put students in small groups and give each group one of the following texts. Their job is to read the book together and then record (or flag, using Post-it Notes) the effective phrases that describe the setting in the story.

Effective Mentor Texts	Setting
Grades 1 to 6	*All the Places to Love* by Patricia MacLachlan *Cloudy with a Chance of Meatballs* by Judi Barrett *If You're Not from the Prairie* by David Bouchard *Immi's Gift* by Karin Littlewood *The Lorax* by Dr. Seuss *Owl Moon* by Jane Yolen *SkySisters* by Jan Bourdeau Waboose *Uptown* by Bryan Collier
Grades 5 to 6	*Train to Somewhere* by Eve Bunting

Near the end of our work on setting, I provide each of my students with a post-card. I challenge them to write a story that takes place in the setting on the post-card. The story must include a beginning, middle, and end. The good copy of the entire story must be written on the back of the postcard. Students are forced to be brief. This activity helps them focus on organization and structure, and include the details of the setting within their story. Challenging but fun!

Differentiation to Support Creativity

As is evident by the extensive teaching necessary for narrative writing, one short unit will not suffice. Exploring the concepts of plot patterns, narrative structure, dialogue, character development, and setting should be spread throughout the year for maximum effectiveness. And because narrative writing is a creative process, it is necessary to differentiate for the needs of our students.

Most important, be flexible in your teaching of narrative writing. Though you teach students to make a story plan or character web, understand that it may not be something all students find useful or even necessary. Students should be expected to complete the assignments on these concepts as you teach them, but later, when they are engaged in writing their narratives, allow them to choose one of the options that work best for them. If a student seems stifled by a story plan but can produce excellent stories, don't suppress her creativity by forcing the plan. If a student benefits from talking out his story beforehand, provide this opportunity with an adult or peer. There is no need (or room) for conformity when it comes to the creative process. Consider your ultimate goal.

To wake up the creative brain, use freewriting as a warm-up for your class as they begin their narrative writing for the day. For example, say, "Write about the breakfast you ate this morning" (two or three minutes only). Then, immediately after, say, "Write about the breakfast you *wish* you ate this morning" (again, two or three minutes only). These types of activities help students add detail to their story writing and tend to stimulate our students' creativity.

Excite students even further by adding items to your Inspiration Station (introduced in Chapter 1). Purchase one of the various flipbooks that allow students to create combinations of characters in various situations. There are also many foam cubes available for story starters. Those developed for very young students

A Grade 2 teacher who had just tried freewriting with her class for the first time came up to me excitedly. "It actually works!" she said. "All of them were writing! And they were excited about it!"
Capitalize on the effect of freewriting even as you set out to write narrative stories.

My favorite flipbook is *Write about Story Starters* by McDonald Publishing.

use pictures rather than words. Young students can either tell an oral story or begin writing a simple story. Sets of cubes with words (characters, setting, problems) are more appropriate for older students. You could even make your own. Be sure to include a baby name book for students looking for character names.

Expand your Inspiration Station even further. Some students may need to create physically before they can create on paper. As Angela Stockman (2016) suggests in *Make Writing*,

> That kid who claims to hate writing may be a maker, and making could become his gateway to writing. Makers are imaginative: They construct entire worlds inside of their minds, and they long to bring them to life by creating tangible prototypes and products. They are passionate do-it-yourselfers who learn by building, who tinker as they go, and who iterate from failure. (15)

If this sounds like some of your students, then be sure to provide options for the way their minds work. Do they need puppets, playdough, or blocks to work out the details of their writing? Could Minecraft be the "buy-in" to get a particular student to write? Although some teachers worry that their classrooms will be turned into playrooms, ultimately, if our students are writing, we should honor and support their processes. If we talk openly with students about processes, they may test out various methods, but eventually, they will figure out and gravitate towards what works for them as individuals.

By providing options and creating a classroom full of ideas, I rarely have students say they do not know what to write about. Instead, their questions and comments have become much more literary: "Okay, I'm working on my transformation story but I'm not sure if my transforming event is convincing enough." "Do you think my character is believable?" "When you read this, do you get a clear picture of my setting?"

Wouldn't you appreciate hearing questions like these from your students?

Provide a Real Audience

If I spent hours planning, writing, and revising a story, I would want to share it with others! The same is true for our students. Provide an audience for your students in some form or another.

- Introduce the idea of an author's chair, where students can read their work to their peers.
- Display student writing in the classroom for others to read and enjoy. When students are reading independently in class, give them the option of choosing a piece of writing by a peer from a bulletin board or basket.
- Enable students to share their stories with a buddy class.
- If your class has pen pals, send copies of the stories as a surprise. (Arrange this with the teacher beforehand to ensure that your students get a response in return.)
- Write stories to be shared with seniors. Consider delivering the stories personally to a seniors' home.
- Invite parents to a publishing party! Serve cookies and juice. Students will share their revised and polished stories with their parents.

Selective Assessment

Just as with freewriting, I do not assess every story my students write.

It is important to note that I do not have my students take all of their stories to a final draft. As we learn more about narrative structure, dialogue, character and setting, I often have students revisit a story they have already written to improve on it with the new skills they have learned. Our students would cringe if we asked them to revise and edit (and worse yet, recopy) every story they wrote. More and more schools have technology readily at their students' fingertips. Regardless, though, it is work to revise and edit!

Every so often, I expect my students to pick one of their favorite stories to spend time editing and revising. I use the 6 + 1 Writing Rubric for assessing narrative writing and students become very familiar with the rubric. The rubric focuses on six qualities of good writing: ideas, organization, voice, word choice, sentence fluency, and conventions (see Chapter 3 for more information on the 6 + 1 traits of writing). Before I assess their stories, students meet with their writing groups and then use the feedback of their peers when making edits and revisions.

I sometimes provide the writing groups with a specific task depending on what our emphasis has been in class. For example: "Today your focus is on setting. Does the writer paint a clear picture in our minds? Give some examples of the phrases that describe the setting." After meeting with their writing groups, students revise, edit, and eventually take the story to its final stage.

I only assess narrative writing that has gone through the revision process.

If you decide to teach your students to use words other than *said*, also teach them not to avoid the word altogether. A balance is key.

During the teaching of various components of narrative writing (e.g., dialogue, character development, and setting), I ask students to look at the rubric and tell me which sections will be affected if we improve whatever it is we are focusing on. With dialogue, for example, students eventually realize that improved dialogue will help in every section of our rubric. The content will improve because student writing will include a balance of dialogue and description. The organization may improve because the students choose to use dialogue to write an effective opening. The sentence structure will improve because students will use dialogue tags at the beginning, in the middle, and at the end of their sentences, therefore, making their sentences a variety of lengths and formats. The vocabulary will improve because they will be using other words besides *said*. The use of conventions will improve because they will ensure they have proper quotation marks and end punctuation. By engaging in these discussions about the rubric, students are motivated to improve their writing.

Another way to assess our students' writing without stifling student work is to assess only one component of the writing. For example, if the focus has been on character development in transformation stories, I assess only that aspect of the student writing. Or, if our focus has been on stuck stories, then I might assess only content and organization. As a teacher, I find that this approach saves an enormous amount of time and yet still serves the desired purpose.

Five line masters pertaining to plot outlines discussed in this chapter follow: Transformation Story, Stuck Story, Circle Story, Competition Story, and Quest Story.

Transformation Story

Characteristics after change occurs:

Character actions after change occurs:

Transforming Event

Characteristics before change occurs:

Character actions before change occurs:

Name of character: _____

Title of story: _____

Author: _____

Pembroke Publishers © 2017 *How Do I Get Them to Write?* by Karen Filewych ISBN 978-1-55138-322-4

Stuck Story

Title of story: _____

Author: _____

What (or who) gets stuck?

Where does it get stuck?

What do the characters do to try to get it unstuck?

1. _____

2. _____

3. _____

What finally works to get it unstuck?

Circle Story

Title of story: _____

Author: _____

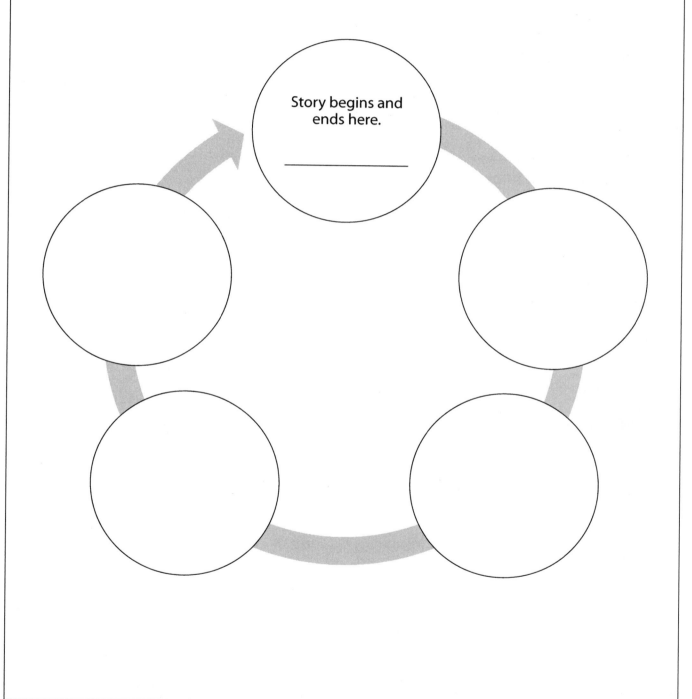

Story begins and
ends here.

_____

Pembroke Publishers © 2017 *How Do I Get Them to Write?* by Karen Filewych ISBN 978-1-55138-322-4

Competition Story

Title of story: _____

Author: _____

Who is competing?

What kind of competition is it?

What are they competing for?

Who wins? How?

Pembroke Publishers © 2017 *How Do I Get Them to Write?* by Karen Filewych ISBN 978-1-55138-322-4

Quest Story

Title of story: _____

Author: _____

Who is on a quest?

What are they searching for?

What does the main character do to find what he/she is looking for?

What obstacles does the character face?

1. _____

2. _____

3. _____

How does the character reach the goal?

Pembroke Publishers © 2017 *How Do I Get Them to Write?* by Karen Filewych ISBN 978-1-55138-322-4

7
Transactional Writing

"I wish we could change the world by creating powerful writers for forever instead of just indifferent writers for school."
— Mem Fox

Few of our students will write narratives beyond the school setting; most, though, will write to communicate — to persuade, enlighten, convince, or motivate. Transactional writing is seen as a more functional form of writing than narrative writing: it is writing that students *will* do outside the school setting, writing that can empower them in our literate-dependent society. So, rather than creating fictitious events or inventing situations, it is important for us to provide students with authentic scenarios whenever possible.

I experienced the power of an authentic scenario first-hand when teaching Grade 6. We had visited the Alberta legislature and the students were disgusted with the arrogance and disrespect the members displayed to one another during the assembly. Perhaps the breaking point came when one student dropped his paper, and another bent down to hand it back to him. They quietly and respectfully exchanged a few words, and the security officer in the gallery came over and reprimanded them for speaking. Simultaneously, blatant heckling, interruption, and disrespect echoed from the assembly below.

Relevant Writing for Real Audiences

"Giving unreal writing activities to our students is about as useful as giving occupational therapy for stroke victims to people who are in perfect health." — Mem Fox (1993, 4)

When we arrived back to class, the students, sparked to "do something," decided to write a letter. I was simply their scribe as they passionately wrote a powerful letter to the Premier, the Speaker of the House, and the members of the Legislative Assembly. I had warned them that they might not receive a response; however, they received several, including a visit from the Leader of the Opposition. The Speaker of the House read their letter to the Legislative Assembly, and we were told that from then on all school groups would be introduced and acknowledged in the Alberta legislature. These students realized their role in the social world and the power of language when channelled productively.

The power of my Grade 6 class's writing stemmed from the passion and disillusionment of the moment. This scenario was student initiated, authentic, and sparked by emotion; it thus provided motivation for students to write. Using provocative, relevant, and authentic experiences can, indeed, motivate our students. "When we are interested in what we are learning," writes Dennis Littky (2004,

98), "no one has to force us to keep learning; we just do." Allow student interest to guide the reading and writing experiences in your classroom.

Realistically, of course, we cannot always wait for students to suggest a writing assignment. Read your local newspapers and watch for stories or events that could become the cornerstone of your language arts program. In our city, for example, Lucy is an elephant who has drawn much controversy over the years. She is now the lone elephant at the zoo and some animal rights groups feel that she should be moved to a sanctuary. Many others are in opposition, arguing that the move would be detrimental to her health. Even for very young children, this is an opportunity for debate and authentic writing experiences. It is an issue that the students connect with on an emotional level and many students even have personal stories about their visits to the zoo.

In exemplary classrooms, students spend their language arts time actively engaged in meaningful and authentic reading and writing activities. Let student interest be your guide. Tony Stead's book *Is That a Fact?* is an excellent resource for teaching all types of nonfiction writing. As Stead says, "What we as teachers must do is help children discover what the types of nonfiction writing look like and the structures and features that competent writers use when writing for specific purposes" (2002, 11).

When I teach transactional writing, I build from letter writing to basic opinion pieces to persuasive pieces, to expository and then eventually, to article writing. They are very much connected though distinct forms of writing. I do not usually teach article writing until Grades 5 and 6.

Notes on Rubric Use for Assessment

When assessing transactional writing, I use rubrics developed for each form of writing. Instead of using a full rubric and risking that my students will find it overwhelming, I tend to focus on specific elements for each of the forms. The 6 + 1 Rubrics could also be used in their place. If you teach in a jurisdiction with provincial/state testing that includes some form of writing, consider using the rubric provided to ensure that students become accustomed to it.

As with narrative writing, my students become very familiar with the rubrics we use in transactional writing. Students should be able to assess their own work and use the information on the rubrics to improve it before the assignment is assessed by you as teacher. As always, assessment is meant to be a tool to improve their writing, not simply a final mark for a report card.

To make the use of rubrics more meaningful for students, you can show an exemplar of the genre you are currently working on and assess it together. A second exemplar can then be used for students to assess on their own or in their writing groups. By the time they are about to write and then to self-assess their work, students will be familiar with the expectations on the rubric.

As you teach the various genres of writing to your students, save some copies of each to use as exemplars. It is helpful to keep a range of exemplars on hand (not all of the same ability) to use with students in future years. I always ask the permission of my students and let them know that their names will never be shared. Most students are eager to oblige!

For details, visit www.canadapost.ca/santa. Specific information is available in the months leading up to Christmas.

Letter Writing

For our very young students, the months leading up to Christmas are the perfect time to begin writing letters. If you live in Canada, Santa is just waiting for your students' letters. In fact, if you send them early enough, he will even respond.

Consider keeping a copy of each of the student letters, or simply use this motivating reason to write as an opportunity to teach the format of a letter.

The benefit of this form of writing is that students see it as authentic: their letters will be read by someone other than the teacher. To capitalize on this natural motivation, find a pen-pal class across the city or across the world. If you know a teacher at another school, ask if he or she would be willing to teach letter writing at the same time. Then, pair up your students as pen pals. This opportunity becomes an ongoing reason to write and discuss the writing process. Students often treat their work with more care when they know that the audience is real. Writing to pen pals also enables you to discuss things such as tone and tact.

There are many options for letter writing. Provide newspapers and engage in discussion about current events in your classroom. What are your students inspired by in the world? What provokes or upsets them? Who can they write to? A government official? An organization? The other classes within the school? The local art gallery? A restaurant? A grandparent? A former teacher or camp counsellor? Watch for those moments, like my field trip to the legislature, that emotionally stir your students. Do not stifle their emotion but, instead, channel it into a powerful learning experience.

Are you looking for something new for parent-teacher-student conferences or your demonstrations of learning? Have your students prepare a letter to their parents that will be on their desks when the parents arrive. Try this prompt as a freewrite: "You may be surprised to know that in school I ..." Students can generate the content during a freewrite and then organize the ideas into letter format afterwards. This task encourages much discussion and revision about effective letter writing. When parents arrive for their parent-teacher-student conference, encourage them to write a sentence or two in return. Again, the activity becomes writing for an authentic purpose.

And although letter writing is a functional task, there is a place for creativity, personality, and voice. Sometimes, we ask students to create cards or letters for a guest speaker or sick classmate. Instead of treating this as a rushed extra task, take the time to make it a learning opportunity by talking about purpose and audience. What message are we trying to convey? What would a hurried, sloppy card communicate? On the other hand, what message is conveyed by a card created with care and thought about the person receiving it?

Teach your students to format their letters using five simple components: the date, a greeting (Dear _____,), the body, a closing, and a signature. Within the body of the letter, students need to include three paragraphs (beginning, middle, and end). If you are mailing the letter, model how to include the address or simply put the address on the envelope and not on the letter. If you do expect the format to include addresses, post a sample as a reference for students. There is no reason for students to memorize the format especially when a quick Internet search provides guidance on form. A simple format and appropriate content are more important to me at the elementary level.

If you teach Grade 4, 5, or 6 and plan to teach letter writing, consider reading *Extra Credit* by Andrew Clements to your class first. The novel is about an American girl and a boy from Afghanistan who become pen pals.

While you may be tempted to have students write "practice" letters, as much as possible, arrange for them to write letters for authentic audiences. The practice will occur through the guided writing experiences.

These books are an entertaining introduction to letter writing; however, they do not necessarily follow the letter writing format we teach our students.

Effective Mentor Texts	Letter Writing
Grades 1 to 6	*The Day the Crayons Quit* by Drew Daywalt *The Day the Crayons Came Home* by Drew Daywalt *Dear Mrs. LaRue: Letters from Obedience School* by Mark Teague *The Jolly Postman or Other People's Letters* by Janet and Allan Ahlberg *Meerkat Mail* by Emily Gravatt
Grades 4 to 6	*Extra Credit* by Andrew Clements *The Gardener* by Sarah Stewart

Letter Writing	Exceeds Expectations 5	Meets Expectations 3	Below Expectations 1
Organization	Letter is written in three paragraphs with an effective beginning, middle, and end.	Letter includes a beginning, middle, and end.	Letter shows little organization.
Audience	Tone and content are appropriate for the target audience.	Tone and content are mostly appropriate for the target audience.	Tone and content are not appropriate for the target audience.
Formatting	Letter includes all of the following: date, greeting, body, closing, and signature.	Letter includes three or four of the following: date, greeting, body, closing, signature.	Letter includes one or two of the following: date, greeting, body, closing, and signature.
Conventions	Errors, if present, do not interrupt flow and effectiveness.	Errors sometimes interrupt flow and effectiveness.	Errors significantly reduce flow and effectiveness.

Opinion Pieces

Before your students begin writing opinion pieces, teach a few mini-lessons on fact and opinion. Students will need to use both in their writing and it is important that they distinguish between the two. *Duck! Rabbit!* by Amy Krouse Rosenthal and Tom Lichtenheld is my favorite way to begin the unit: it generates an engaging and often hilarious discussion. *The True Story of the Three Little Pigs* by Jon Scieszka is another fun book to continue the discussion on fact and opinion.

After reading appropriate literature, the students and I write one or two freewrites with prompts such as "I think …", "I feel …", "I believe …" or even "Everyone should …" After writing, ask students to look through their freewriting and determine what they wrote more of: fact or opinion? Typically, of course, in this type of writing we are focusing on our opinions. Students can now be shown how to support their opinions with facts by adding details.

Through these freewrite prompts, students will begin to focus on topics they are passionate about. For example, in a freewrite prompted by "I believe ...," a student may have written about seven different things. But perhaps after reading the freewrite back to herself she realizes that there is one statement or portion of her freewrite that she feels strongly about and wants to focus on for her opinion piece. This then becomes her topic for the upcoming writing assignment.

When you teach your students to write opinion pieces, keep the format simple. I post this structure for students to reference throughout the process.

1. State your opinion in one or two sentences.
2. Back up your opinion with reasons.
3. Wrap up your argument in one or two sentences.

Determine the desired length of the reasons portion of the piece based on the age level and ability of your students.

When teaching students to write their opening sentences, encourage them to be creative. They could begin with a question or a surprising fact. For example, a student intent on expressing the idea that red is the best color in the universe might begin with *Did you know that Crayola Crayon makes 23 shades of red, more shades than any other color? Red simply must be the best.* A student writing to express that hockey is the best sport might begin with something like this: *He shoots, he scores!*

I tend to gravitate to the following simple, straightforward assignment when teaching students to write opinion pieces: write about your favorite color, animal, or sport. *Red Is Best* and *Chameleons Are Cool* are effective literature references. This assignment is engaging for students of all ages, including Grade 1. I have found that some students find it easier to write opinion pieces if they are comparing two things: red is better than blue, dogs are better than cats, hockey is better than soccer. Students could also write an opinion piece about a favorite food, movie, video game, toy, or book. Or, they may have discovered their topic within a freewrite. If students are provided with a choice in topic, they are more likely to be engaged in the writing process.

Effective Mentor Texts	Opinion Pieces
Grades 1 to 3	*Chameleons Are Cool* by Martin Jenkins *Duck! Rabbit!* by Amy Krouse Rosenthal and Tom Lichtenheld *Earrings!* by Judith Viorst *Red Is Best* by Kathy Stinson *Too Many Toys* by David Shannon
Grades 4 to 6	*Animals Nobody Loves* by Seymour Simon *Brave Irene* by William Steig *The Popcorn Book* by Tomie de Paola *The True Story of the Three Little Pigs* by Jon Scieszka

Opinion Pieces	Exceeds Expectations 5	Meets Expectations 3	Below Expectations 1
Ideas and Content	Opinion is clearly stated. Opinion is effectively supported by many details.	Opinion is fairly clear. Opinion is supported by some details.	Opinion is not clear. Opinion is not supported with detail.

As always, introduce the rubric to students early on in the teaching of opinion pieces. They should always know what they are working towards.

Organization	Writing includes a strong beginning, middle, and end. Transitions are effective.	Writing includes a beginning, middle, and end. Some transitions are used.	Writing is disorganized with no obvious beginning, middle, and end.
Voice	Writing reflects the writer's personality. Point of view is evident. Writing is lively and expressive.	Writing attempts to reflect the personality of the writer. Point of view is present. Writing is somewhat expressive.	Writing does not reflect the writer's personality. Point of view is lacking. Writing is not expressive.
Conventions	Errors, if present, do not interrupt flow and effectiveness.	Errors sometimes interrupt flow and effectiveness.	Errors significantly reduce flow and effectiveness.

Persuasive Writing

Begin your persuasive writing discussion by reading aloud the Dr. Seuss classic *Green Eggs and Ham*. The entire book is an attempt at persuasion. Teachers of older students sometimes balk at reading what they deem too childish for their students. Students of all grades will be open to picture books, however, if you set them up as mentor texts and use them routinely. And though they may be reluctant to admit it, students tend to enjoy these picture book read-alouds.

Persuasive writing is very much connected to opinion pieces. Whereas in opinion pieces the goal is to clearly communicate their opinions, in persuasive writing, students are trying to persuade someone to do something. There is a stakeholder involved. An opinion piece might speak to the benefits (or disadvantages) of school uniforms; a persuasive writing piece might be a letter to the principal or the parent council as the school is considering bringing in school uniforms. An opinion piece might describe a favorite animal; a persuasive writing piece might be an effort to convince a parent to buy a pet.

Guided Writing

The students and I often write our first persuasive piece together. I begin by reading them *A Fine, Fine School* by Sharon Creech. In this book, the principal loves school so much that he decides everyone should come to school on Saturdays. He considers it such a success that he decides everyone must also come on Sundays, then on holidays, and even during the summer. After we have read this book together, I ask the students to imagine that the principal in the book is actually our principal. We must write to him to persuade him not to make us come to school on all of these extra days. The students are eager to begin; therefore, this is the perfect opportunity to introduce the idea of counter-arguments and then to teach the format of a persuasive piece.

One way to assist students in pushing their persuasion piece beyond that of an opinion piece is to help them consider counter-arguments. During this discussion, continue using the idea from the book *A Fine, Fine School*. Ask the students why the principal Mr. Keene wants more days of school. Jot down their ideas on the board as they contribute. After they have identified all of his reasons, write the students' counter-arguments on the board next to each. This is a simple way to help the students understand the concept. Even our young students can deal with it with some support and dialogue.

Coming Up with Counter-Arguments

What might a counter-argument consist of? Assume that students are writing to persuade their parents to buy them a pet. They might anticipate that the parents will say the cost is too high. The counter-argument for the students could be that they will give up their allowances, birthday gifts, and Christmas presents. They also might research the local humane society where they could adopt an animal at a low cost. They would then include these details in their writing.

Older students might be involved in more complicated counter-arguments. If arguing *against* school uniforms, they should try to anticipate an argument *for* school uniforms and address it within their writing. For example, someone who wants school uniforms might say that the uniforms will reduce the competitiveness or comparisons between students. The student might then argue that maintaining individual choice in clothing will better prepare students for the "real world" because it is a more accurate reflection of what they will face in society. As you can see, this form of writing requires students to demonstrate higher-level thinking skills, such as analyzing and evaluating.

Encourage students to follow the same format as they did for opinion pieces. The difference this time is the language used to persuade the reader.

1. State your opinion in one or two sentences.
2. Back up your opinion with reasons (length to be determined based on the age level and ability of the students).
3. Wrap up your argument in one or two sentences.

Now that the students know the format, write a persuasive piece together convincing your principal *not* to have school every day of the week. It can even be fun to prep your principal and assistant principal about this assignment. If they know what your class is up to, they may play along.

Determining a Topic for Persuasion

In the days following this guided writing experience, challenge the students to come up with their own topic for a persuasive piece. Some teachers prefer to have all students write on the same topic. I prefer to have the class brainstorm ideas together and then let each student choose a topic. During this planning stage of persuasive writing, it can be helpful for students to meet in their writing groups and share their topics. They can discuss the various opinions about the topics and assist one another in developing counter-arguments.

What to write about? Likely there are things within your school that your students might want to change: the amount of homework, the length of recess, or even a school rule. The principal, or even you as the teacher, could be the stake-holder that the students would be trying to convince of the change.

What are your students' interests? Football, animals, airplanes, recycling? How could these interests spark a "real" writing experience? Consider perusing the newspaper for ideas. For example, there is an increasingly vocal debate about concussions in sports. Perhaps you have a student who feels strongly that rules should be changed in football leagues to prevent concussions: he could write to the local community league or football association about the topic. He suddenly has an authentic purpose. A student who loves animals might write to encourage people to adopt a pet. A student who is enthusiastic about protecting the environment could write to convince readers to use public transportation rather than cars. A student who is passionate about recycling could write to persuade the community to do more recycling. A little creative thinking can generate a persuasive writing piece for most topics.

Sometimes, I throw a twist into an assignment on persuasive writing. I may ask students to take the opinion opposite of their own and then persuade the reader to accept this point of view. This task pushes our students to think beyond their own perspectives. It encourages some research and often yields very strong writing.

Examine your curriculum in other subject areas. Consider topics in science and social studies. The science curriculum and care for the environment provide many excellent possible topic ideas, for example, pollution, idling, global warming, and appropriate water use. Is there a particular region you study? In Alberta, our Grade 2 students study Communities in Canada. They learn about and compare Inuit, Acadian, and prairie communities. In one case, the Grade 2 classes in our school had to write a persuasive piece convincing their family to move to Iqaluit, the capital of Nunavut. They had learned about the climate, the culture, and the geography of this Northern territory. They used these details when presenting their arguments to their parents. Students engaged in research, had a specific audience in mind, and certainly had a purpose for their writing. All of these factors influenced the quality of their writing.

Effective Mentor Texts	Persuasive Writing
Grades 1 to 6	*A Fine, Fine School* by Sharon Creech *Green Eggs and Ham* by Dr. Seuss *Have I Got a Book for You!* by Mélanie Watt *I Wanna New Room* by Karen Kaufman Orloff *I Wanna Iguana* by Karen Kaufman Orloff *The Perfect Pet* by Margie Palatini *What Pet Should I Get?* by Dr. Seuss

Persuasive Writing	Exceeds Expectations 5	Meets Expectations 3	Below Expectations 1
Ideas and Content	Opinion is clearly stated. Opinion is effectively supported by many details. Writer anticipates counter-arguments and addresses them effectively.	Opinion is fairly clear. Opinion is supported by some details. Writer anticipates some counter-arguments and attempts to address them.	Opinion is not clear. Opinion is not supported with detail. Writer does not anticipate counter-arguments.
Voice	Writing reflects the writer's personality. Point of view is evident. Writing is lively and expressive.	Writing attempts to reflect the personality of the writer. Point of view is present. Writing is somewhat expressive.	Writing does not reflect the writer's personality. Point of view is lacking. Writing is not expressive.
Word Choice	Word choice clearly helps to persuade audience.	Word choice helps to persuade audience.	Word choice does little to persuade audience.
Conventions	Errors, if present, do not interrupt flow and effectiveness.	Errors sometimes interrupt flow and effectiveness.	Errors significantly reduce flow and effectiveness.

Expository Text

If you have not yet had the discussion about the differences between fact and opinion, see "Opinion Pieces," earlier in the chapter.

Nonfiction Text Features: Examples
- Table of contents
- Illustrations
- Maps
- Charts
- Captions
- Titles
- Labels
- Glossary

Now that students understand the difference between fact and opinion, it is time to focus on facts. One of the exciting aspects of teaching students to write expository texts is that they can choose a topic of interest to them: perhaps animals, insects, sports, food, even the weather. A curricular science or social studies topic is often effective because then much of the research is also meeting other outcomes. The final products of expository writing can come in many forms: books, brochures, reports, or diagrams, for example.

Before students begin to write expository texts, show them several book pairings: one fiction and one nonfiction on the same topic. Likely, a look through your bookshelf or a search in your school library will yield a good pairing. For example, hold up *The Little Engine That Could* and any nonfiction book about trains. (Eyewitness, National Geographic, and Usborne all publish excellent nonfiction books for children.) Ask students to predict what the books will be about. Discuss similarities and differences, first of the cover, and eventually the inside pages as you do a picture walk together. Typically, students will realize that one is a story created by an author and the other is a text presenting factual information. Some students will also point out the text features in the nonfiction book.

Take the opportunity to discuss the purpose of the text features. Remember, good readers become good writers. Take the time here to make them good readers!

Possible Book Pairings	
Fiction	**Nonfiction**
The Little Engine That Could by Watty Piper	*Trains* by Amy Shields (National Geographic)
Sylvester and the Magic Pebble by William Steig	*A Rock Is Lively* by Dianna Hutts Aston
Old Turtle by Douglas Wood	*Sea Turtles* by Laura Marsh (National Geographic)
How to Catch a Star by Oliver Jeffers	*Stars: A Family Guide to the Night Sky* by Adam Ford
If You Happen to Have a Dinosaur by Linda Bailey	*DK Eyewitness: Dinosaur* by David Lambert

Before students complete an independent assignment, I spend considerable time guiding them through the various elements necessary to write expository text.

- Choose a topic.
- Brainstorm what you already know about the topic.
- Choose the expository format you wish to create.
- Locate appropriate sources.
- Read and extract information.
- Write your text in a clear and logical way.

With all grade levels, take the time to model the entire process from beginning to end. Choose a topic together (ideally connected to your curriculum) and begin by making either a web or a chart recording the information your students already know about the topic.

Next, read many nonfiction books at your students' ability level and slightly beyond their reading level. Ask students to write some information in their own words as (or after) you read. Watch any related videos, too, and encourage students to record information in the form of jot notes. After each of these research experiences, record student ideas on chart paper and post the sheets around the room so students can refer to them when beginning to write.

After a few days of research — do not hurry the process — begin to write together as a class. Ask students what text features they think they should include and talk through the organization of the piece. Talking through this stage and making a rough outline, or drawing, shows students how to plan what they are going to do. Spend a few days writing, revising, and polishing the work, continuing to garner student feedback and input along the way.

Students are usually quite excited to begin writing their own expository pieces. Now that they have been through the process from beginning to end, it becomes much more manageable for them. With the youngest students, it can be most effective to complete the research portion of the project together (which means a common topic); the student choice comes in the format of the final project.

Students as Researchers

Begin by calling your students "researchers." This again sets an expectation and gives a validity and purpose to what they are doing.

One of the obstacles in teaching students to write expository text based on facts is the research itself. We have all had the experience of watching students copy text directly from a book or the Internet and claim that they are finished. (These moments trigger a timely discussion of plagiarism.) Most often, students, especially the younger ones, do not even realize that there is anything wrong with this. Even worse, they rarely understand what they have written! Our challenge, then, is to teach our students to read and extract information from various sources.

In my experience, the use of a partner is essential in helping students put information into their own words. With a source in front of them (book, magazine, the Internet), I encourage the researcher's partner to read the information out loud. The researcher must then jot down notes from the information being read. Together, they can discuss what the information means.

Utilize sources such as BrainPOP or Discovery Education for the excellent videos on a wide selection of topics. Model the research process and the taking of jot notes. The first time through, watch the complete video (they are typically fairly short) to gain the big picture of the topic. Then, watch again, this time modelling the taking of jot notes as they watch. Pause the video at various points and ask students to summarize what was just said. Then, everyone writes the sentence or phrase you have come up with together. Watch a third time through (without stopping the video) and students can add anything to their notes that they think they have missed.

One of the other obstacles is finding resources at the reading level of the students. Consider alternative sources. Bring in an expert to speak to the students or involve the students' parents. When his students are completing nonfiction projects, Tony Stead sends a letter to their parents, asking for assistance. For example, as part of the letter before a unit of study on ants, he wrote:

> If you have an Internet connection, see what you can find out about ants ...
> We don't want the children to come into the classroom with pages of
> scientific facts that you have simply printed from the Internet. It is far more
> valuable for them to come into the classroom with a few facts they can talk
> about in their own words. (Stead 2002, 42)

Instead of students having pages of information copied from another source, I would rather they have less information but that it be true and in their own words. In elementary school, it is more important to learn the skill of writing information in their own words and less important that students learn how to reference the information. That will come.

Near the end of the research portion of the project, plan time for the students to meet with their writing groups. This time is most effective after students have their research and their plan but before they begin putting information into its final form. This way, they can talk through the information they have gathered, share their plan with their peers, and gather feedback before beginning to write. The peer feedback may guide them in a direction they had not considered on their own. Give them a few days of writing time and then provide students with at least one more session with their writing groups to talk through and share their progress. These sessions will encourage refinement and revision through the constructive critique of their peers.

After so much time and energy have gone into creating this expository writing, be sure to provide your students with an audience for their work. Perhaps you could send two or three of your students to present in each classroom of the school. Or, you may be able to time your project so students can share with their parents during a parent-teacher-student conference. Or, if you have a buddy class, arrange for students to present to their buddies. Regardless of who the audience is, students will appreciate the opportunity to share what they have spent so much time creating!

Expository Text	Exceeds Expectations 5	Meets Expectations 3	Below Expectations 1
Ideas and Content	Information is on topic and extensive. Information is accurate.	Information is on topic and fairly complete. Information is mostly accurate.	Information is limited. Information is not accurate.
Organization/ Format	Ideas are well organized. Appropriate format was chosen to convey information effectively.	Ideas are somewhat organized. Appropriate format was chosen.	Ideas are not organized. Format is unclear or not appropriate for the topic.
Text Features (e.g., illustrations, captions, labels, titles, maps)	Many text features were used to enhance the presentation of the topic.	Some text features were used effectively.	Few or no text features were used.
Word Choice	Words are specific and accurate for the topic. Writer chose words carefully.	Some words are specific and accurate.	It does not appear that words were chosen with the topic in mind.
Conventions	Errors, if present, do not interrupt flow and effectiveness.	Errors sometimes interrupt flow and effectiveness.	Errors significantly reduce flow and effectiveness.

Newspaper Articles

In my province of Alberta, all students in Grade 6 are tested on two forms of writing: narrative and article writing. Article writing involves considerably different skills than other forms. It is a perfect opportunity to teach brevity, clarity, sentence structure, and organization. This form of writing is effective for all upper elementary students as it easily connects to many curricular areas. Students could write articles about a field trip they went on or about events in the school, such as Read In Week. They could write articles about the environment after doing research in science. They could also address current events. Is your local hockey team making a run for the Stanley Cup? Is it election time? Is the city deciding whether to build a bridge? Are the Olympics going on? You can capitalize on such real-world events.

Before writing, engage in a discussion about the purposes of newspaper articles. Students should recognize that the main purpose is to inform. Discuss the necessity for bias-free reporting for news stories and the difference between a typical article and an opinion piece. Consider how the purpose of some articles is also to entertain. Talk, too, about the frequency of newspapers being published (in print or online) and how this may affect the writing.

After this discussion in my class, we spend time reading articles together. We talk about how the language is different than in other forms of writing: typically, sentences are shorter, paragraphs are shorter, the text is very much to the point, and the style is generally more prescribed than in other forms of writing. We observe the word choice in the articles we are reading and look for active verbs and appropriate description.

Exploring the Inverted Pyramid

I then teach the students the 5 Ws: Who, What, Where, When, and Why. We look for (and highlight) the 5 Ws in the articles we read together. We observe how this information is often in the first paragraph and into the second. These details are considered most important and are therefore provided at the beginning of the article. As part of this discussion we examine the *inverted pyramid*: articles are written with the most important information first and the least important or background information last. After we have completed this task together a few times, I send students off in partners with a highlighter and a couple of articles that I have chosen.

The students practise identifying the 5 Ws and then I teach them to write a lead in three ways: a summary lead, a quotation lead, and an anecdotal lead. Using the following fictional information, I show my students three sample leads.

- Oct. 3–7, 2016, Read In Week across Canada
- Penny Hill, children's author, visited Raven School as a guest reader on Oct. 7
- Spoke to Grades 4 to 6 about her latest book, *Better with Butterscotch*, and then read an excerpt
- Students gathered in the library to hear her speak
- Students had prepared questions about the writing process
- Book is about a dog named Butterscotch and her twin owners, Carly and Christopher
- Has written 8 novels for children and 2 picture books
- Lives in Humboldt, Saskatchewan

When giving information in note form such as this, I indicate that they can use all or some of the information depending on what they think is important. Because they are writing a fictional article, I allow them to fabricate a quotation or an anecdote to include either at the beginning or within their articles.

A *summary lead* is just what it sounds like and is probably the most common lead used in articles. It summarizes many (if not all) of the 5 Ws in the opening. A possible summary lead based on this information:

> On Friday, October 7, author Penny Hill entertained the Grades 4 to 6 students at Raven School for Read In Week. She was discussing her new book, Better with Butterscotch.

Students should now be able to identify the 5 Ws with ease. On "Friday, October 7 [*when*], author Penny Hill [*who*] entertained the Grades 4 to 6 students [*what*] at Raven School [*where*] for Read In Week [*why*]. She was discussing her new book, Better with Butterscotch [*what*]."

Using a quotation in the opening sentence can also be effective.

> "Even as a little girl, I wanted to be a writer. With hard work, my dreams have come true," Penny Hill explained to the Grades 4 to 6 students from Raven School.

The other details would then follow.

The third method I teach students is to begin the article with an *anecdote*.

> The Grades 4 to 6 students at Raven School sat on the floor of the library waiting for author Penny Hill. She was greeted with cheers and applause.

News That's Fit to Print

A few years ago I used to give my elementary students the local newspapers to peruse while studying current events and article writing. I am now more selective in what I leave out (rarely is the section on world news appropriate for young eyes). I look for more age-appropriate options, such as teachingkidsnews.com. I can't imagine how a young, developing brain would process some of the stories making news these days. If students do stumble upon a difficult subject, discuss it delicately. Maintain an attitude of assurance and hope.

After writing the lead, students should then determine how to complete the remainder of the inverted pyramid with appropriate supporting details. Doing this takes some practice and I encourage students to talk it through with a partner.

Even though a headline is the first thing the reader reads, I teach my students to write their headlines last. After they become more familiar with the content and can organize it appropriately, I find they are better able to write an effective headline.

With their first written articles in front of them, I walk through the rubric with the students; we discuss each section and they assess themselves. I do not assess this particular article. After writing a second article, following a similar process as the first, I let the students choose one of the two articles to revise, edit, and hand in. Only then do I assess the students' work.

Newspaper Articles	Exceeds Expectations 5	Meets Expectations 3	Below Expectations 1
Headline	Headline captures the reader's attention and accurately describes the content.	Headline describes content.	Headline is unclear or missing.
Lead	Lead captures reader's attention and is effective.	Lead is clear and effective.	Lead is not clear or effective.
Ideas and Content	5 Ws are clearly addressed. Ideas are well developed. Appropriate supporting details are included effectively. All facts are accurate.	Most of the 5 Ws are clearly addressed. Ideas are fairly well developed. Supporting details are appropriate. Most facts are accurate.	Information is missing or inaccurate. Ideas are not explained or developed. Supporting details are missing or inaccurate.

Organization	Use of inverted pyramid is effective with most important information first.	Use of inverted pyramid is adequate.	Use of inverted pyramid is not evident. Information is not organized.
Word Choice	Word choice enhances the article and sets appropriate tone.	Word choice is adequate and appropriate for the article.	Word choice is limited and/or not appropriate for an article.
Conventions	Errors, if present, do not interrupt the flow and effectiveness of article.	Errors sometimes interrupt the flow and effectiveness of article.	Errors significantly reduce the flow and effectiveness of article.

Writing for Real

Transactional writing is easily applied in a variety of subject areas. Perhaps your students want to invite a guest from the planetarium: writing the letter to request the visit is writing for a real purpose and can be done effectively through guided writing. Perhaps your school hosted a market or bake sale to raise money for a social justice initiative: students could write an article describing the event for the school newsletter. If your class or your school requires donations from parents or businesses, the students can craft the letters. Expository writing is also a perfect companion to the science curriculum.

Using these real-writing experiences demonstrates to students how writing is a skill used not only within language arts, not only within the school setting, but beyond the walls of our classrooms. What better lesson can there be?

8

The Playfulness of Poetry

"Painting is silent poetry, and poetry is painting with the gift of speech."
— Simonides

Teachers and students alike are sometimes intimidated by poetry, and yet, when approached intelligently and creatively, it can be one of the most liberating forms of reading and writing for students of all abilities. "[P]oetry reaches to the heart, not the head, of the learner, in a whimsical language that appeals to children" (Cecil 1994, 2). Poetry often captures a universal moment or feeling that brings the reader to a better understanding of what it means to be human. Poetry can enhance an individual's memory, stir the imagination, evoke emotion, and help conjure up imagery. Poetry for children is often humorous and silly. Poetry has the potential to reach even our most reluctant readers and writers.

The poems of Shel Silverstein, Jack Prelutsky, Dennis Lee, and Bruce Lansky are so much fun that students of any age can appreciate them. Many of the poems by Nicola Davies and Jane Yolen are inspired by nature and coupled with beautiful illustrations and photographs. The stories of Dr. Seuss can be enjoyed and examined for their rhythm and rhyme. Even some of the classics and more sophisticated poems are appropriate for children. Neil Waldman has provided stunning illustrations for William Blake's poem "The Tyger," written in 1794. Many poems by Robert Frost, Emily Dickinson, Walt Whitman, E. E. Cummings, and Langston Hughes are also accessible to children.

Your Poetic History

What are your own experiences with poetry? Do you have memories of a parent or grandparent lovingly reading poetry to you as a child? Or, do you continue to have nightmares about your high-school poetry experiences? Whether you realize it or not, your own thoughts and feelings towards poetry will become obvious to students, sometimes with detrimental results. Some teachers avoid poetry entirely because of their own experiences. Others are not sure how to approach poetry with children.

It is important to determine whether you are a reluctant reader of poetry, someone who finds pleasure in the form, or someone who is indifferent to it. By being honest with yourself, you will become more cognizant of your personal feelings towards poetry so you can teach this unit more productively.

If you do not have a positive response towards poetry, it is worth the effort to discover the pleasure it holds. Do not start with Homer's *Iliad* or Chaucer's *Canterbury Tales*. Doing so would likely reinforce your aversion to the form because of the complexity of the text. Instead, start by finding poems you think your students will enjoy. Try "The Loser" by Shel Silverstein or "Alligator Pie" by Dennis Lee. These poems are fun and accessible to people of all ages.

I have heard many people — both adults and children — articulate that they just don't understand poetry. And though our instincts might be to seek understanding as we do with other genres, it is important to let our students know that it is enough to let poetry move us: to make us laugh or cry, to inspire us, to nudge us to reflect on our lives. We should give ourselves and our students permission to allow poetry to be an experience of emotion rather than of the intellect. In *Saved by a Poem: The Transformative Power of Words*, Kim Rosen (2009) suggests,

> As you read poems, listen to them, and speak them aloud, try meeting them as you would a piece of music. Allow your rational brain to relax. Dare to not understand, to lose your grip on making sense of the words. Let the images, like musical notes, pour over you. (p. xvi)

Finding Delight in Poetry

It is not essential to analyze every word of every poem. We can enjoy poetry simply because of its rhythm and cadence. We can enjoy it because of the commonality of experience. We can enjoy it because of the emotion it stirs in us. Very young children approach poetry in this way instinctively. They don't consider analyzing the poems: they simply find delight in the form. Some of our older students may have preconceived notions about poetry similar to those notions of many adults. These students may assume that poetry is difficult to read and understand. They may not realize the diversity in length, style, or topic. They may not be aware of the playfulness of the form. Therefore, be deliberate in the poetry you choose to share with your students, especially at the beginning of the unit. Be sure to talk to them about experiencing the form through emotion rather than intellect. The intent is to entice the students into the world of poetry.

After students have experienced some delight with poetry, you can then begin to introduce poems with more serious themes or more formal language. Together you can explore how poets take a topic such as nature, life, love or loss and tackle deep emotion with deceiving simplicity. Poems of this more serious nature can help students learn empathy and grasp the wonders of life.

I typically teach poetry over the course of three to four weeks. April is National Poetry Month so I tend to teach it during this time. And although I teach it as a unit then and we are immersed in it, I don't shy away from it at other times of the year. I include it in my regular teaching, as well.

On the next page is a list of recommended poetry resources to read and share with your students.

Poems of Deep Emotion
- "Dust of Snow" by Robert Frost
- *The Elders Are Watching* by David Bouchard
- "Earth Day" by Jane Yolen
- "Hope is the thing with feathers" by Emily Dickinson
- "If" by Rudyard Kipling

Poetry Resource List	
Grades 1 to 6	*Alligator Pie* by Dennis Lee *BookSpeak! Poems about Books* by Laura Purdie Salas *Canadian Poems for Canadian Kids* edited by Jen Hamilton *A Child's Garden of Verses* by Robert Louis Stevenson *The Elders Are Watching* by David Bouchard *Falling Down the Page: A Book of List Poems* edited by Georgia Heard *Forgive Me, I Meant to Do It: False Apology Poems* by Gail Carson Levine *Here's a Little Poem: A Very First Book of Poetry* compiled by Jane Yolen and Andrew Fusek Peters *It's Raining Pigs & Noodles* by Jack Prelutsky *Jelly Belly* by Dennis Lee *Joyful Noise: Poems for Two Voices* by Paul Fleischman *A Light in the Attic* by Shel Silverstein *Love That Dog* by Sharon Creech *A Mirror to Nature* by Jane Yolen *Name That Dog* by Peggy Archer *The New Kid on the Block* by Jack Prelutsky *Noisy Poems for a Busy Day* by Robert Heidbreder *Outside Your Window* by Nicola Davies *Poems to Learn by Heart* by Caroline Kennedy *Poetry for Young People: Animal Poems* *Poetry for Young People: Edgar Allan Poe* *Poetry for Young People: Edward Lear* *Poetry for Young People: Emily Dickinson* *Poetry for Young People: Langston Hughes* *Poetry for Young People: Maya Angelou* *Poetry for Young People: Robert Browning* *Poetry for Young People: Robert Frost* *Poetry for Young People: Rudyard Kipling* *Poetry for Young People: William Shakespeare* edited by David Scott Kastan and Marina Kastan *The Random House Book of Poetry for Children* compiled by Jack Prelutsky *Rolling in the Aisles: A Collection of Laugh-Out-Loud Poems* by Bruce Lansky *Stardines Swim High across the Sky: And Other Poems* by Jack Prelutsky *The Swamps of Sleethe: Poems from beyond the Solar System* by Jack Prelutsky *Switching On the Moon: A Very First Book of Bedtime Poems* by Jane Yolen *The Tyger* by William Blake (Neil Waldman, illustrator) *Water Music: Poems for Children* by Jane Yolen *Where the Sidewalk Ends* by Shel Silverstein *Winter Bees and Other Poems of the Cold* by Joyce Sidman *Winter Poems* selected by Barbara Rogasky *You Wait until I'm Older Than You!* by Michael Rosen

Week 1: Create a Positive Poetry Experience

Begin your unit by reading poetry aloud and enjoying it together. Surround your students with poetry books and give them time to read and explore on their own. Beyond that, discuss the connection between poetry and music. Find the lyrics of your students' favorite songs and explore them for their verse and rhythm.

Sharing of a Favorite Poem

Many students are initially daunted by the idea of presenting a poem, but they enjoy it so much that they later choose a second poem to share.

One of the first assignments I give my students during this unit is to find a favorite poem and prepare to read or recite it to the class. Rosen (2009) intimates, "Poetry was created to be experienced in the body and spoken aloud. Made of breath, sound, rhythm, meaning, and silence, a poem is a physical event. It needs a human body to give it life" (1). By giving students the choice of reading or reciting the favorite poem, students who are intimidated by the thought of memorizing can still be successful: they can practise and read their poem with meaning and expression.

The students could also prepare to recite or read the poem to another class. Ask your colleagues if they would mind having two or three visitors; spreading your class throughout the school ensures you will not burden or inconvenience any one class and host classes are sure to enjoy their guest presenters. Your students will also be excited to prepare for a real audience.

This beginning exploration leads naturally to a conversation about what poetry is and is not. As your students share their thoughts, take the opportunity to challenge any misconceptions that arise. For example, some students might say that poetry must rhyme. Others might believe that it is always short. It can be helpful to have examples on hand to demonstrate the diversity of the form. By spending time engaged in this conversation, your students will begin to see how extensive and liberating this form of reading and writing can be. To assist with this discussion, read *Love That Dog* by Sharon Creech. This novel, about a boy who resists the poetry assignment given by his teacher, is written in the form of a poem. It is a short but amusing read and will tackle many of the trepidations your students might have about poetry.

Websites to Visit
- www.jackprelutsky.com
- www.shelsilverstein.com
- www.poetry4kids.com

Not only will your students enjoy exploring these sites, but there are also many ideas and resources for teachers.

An engaging way to kick off the unit is by inviting a local poet to speak to your students, read to your students, and perhaps even help with the writing process! If it is not feasible to do this then explore a favorite poet's website. Some poets include videos of poetry readings or suggestions for children writing poetry.

Choral Reading

Excellent selections for this purpose include "Homework! Oh, Homework!" by Jack Prelutsky and "Sick" by Shel Silverstein.

Consider preparing a poem for a choral reading experience. Divide up the lines of the poem: some lines will be read by three or four students, some by all girls, and some by all boys. The lines of emphasis might be read by the whole class or by only one student. Involve your students in the discussion about how each line should be read. What do they think is important in this poem? How should it be read? Which lines should be emphasized? Then, practise, practise, and practise some more before performing your choral reading for other classes. I have done this with students as young as Grade 1 and as old as Grade 6. Students of all ages enjoy the experience, and the discussion generated is fascinating.

Topic Lists for Inspiration

During this first week of exploration, begin generating a list of topics that your students encounter in the poetry they read. Leave the list in a visible spot throughout the unit to ensure that they are reminded of the possibilities when it is time to write. Be sure that your list includes straightforward topics such as pets, sports, homework, television, and food. Include events such as a birthday party, playoff game day, Halloween, and the first day of school. Include more abstract topics such as friendship, pain, courage, love, and loss, as well. These lists will provide inspiration to your students throughout the unit and remind them that poetry can truly be about anything!

Beyond suggesting topics, students can help you create a list of first-line prompts, such as these:

- Yesterday I woke up with a superpower.
- I have a secret …
- If my dog could talk …
- When I get old …
- When I was bit by a snake …
- I love to eat …
- I reached into my pocket …
- At the party …
- I'm not good at …
- I have a little problem.

Notice that this first week is not about writing poetry. That will come. The goal of this first week is to inspire your students. Read and immerse yourselves in poetry and tap into the interests and dynamics of your group of students. Have fun with language during this first week of exploration.

Week 2: Teach Various Forms

After surrounding my students with poetry and letting them enjoy the playful language, I then introduce them to at least two new forms of poetry each day. My favorites to use with children are haiku, tanka, list poems, cinquain, limerick, sound poems, found poems, shape poems, acrostic poems, pantoum, and free verse. (See the double-page spread beginning on page 102 for detail.) If the day's focus is the limerick, together the class reads various limericks and then the students write one or two of their own. We do the same with another form, following the same process.

While my students are writing, I target those students who might be somewhat reluctant or intimidated by the form and work closely with them to ensure that they experience success. As with freewriting, my students know they do not have to share every poem they write. This knowledge allows them to be more open to the process and to take greater risks within their writing. Though I always remind them that they are not obliged to share, they tend to be so enthusiastic about their work that they beg to do so. Most often, the energy in the room is high with excitement as they take pleasure in choosing just the right words.

Be aware of any students who might be reluctant to share their work and create the partnerships carefully.

Each day after we have spent time writing, I ask students to meet with their poetry partners. Poetry partners will share their poems with each other throughout the writing process. The poetry partner becomes a trusted peer that a student can turn to for guidance, opinions, or feedback.

Accessible Forms of Poetry for Children

Haiku is a Japanese form of poetry consisting of three lines: Line 1 — 5 syllables; Line 2 — 7 syllables; Line 3 — 5 syllables. In Japanese tradition, haikus are written about nature.

> The crisp mountain air,
> Glacier lakes, blue and vibrant,
> Trees, reaching skyward.

Tanka is a Japanese form much like Haiku but with more lines and syllables. The first three lines are identical to Haiku; then there are two more lines, each with seven syllables. Tanka often uses simile, metaphor, and personification. The form dates back 1200 years.

> Wind, rustling and cool.
> Slowly falling from the trees:
> Brown, yellow, orange, red
> Fall leaves of every color.
> Creating nature's artwork.

A **list poem** is a list of items, people, places, or ideas. It often involves repetition. There may be rhyme or not. A list can be written first and then shaped into a poem with a beginning and an end. For example, "Sick" by Shel Silverstein begins with "I cannot go to school today" and ends with "You say today is ... Saturday? G'bye, I'm going out to play!" In between is a long list of ailments!

A **cinquain** is a five-line poem following a set pattern: Line 1 — a noun; Line 2 — 2 adjectives; Line 3 — 3 verbs ending in *-ing*; Line 4 — a phrase; and Line 5 — a synonym for the noun.

> Video game
> Awesome, cool
> Running, jumping, pounding
> In another world
> Super Mario

A **limerick**, like a cinquain, is a five-line poem, but it is humorous. The limericks of Edward Lear are well known. The first line usually begins with "There was a ..." and ends with a name, person, or place. Lines 1, 2, and 5 each have 7 to 10 syllables; Lines 3 and 4 have 5 to 7 syllables. The rhyme scheme is *aabba*.

A **sound poem** describes sounds we hear around us every day. It might be full of words such as *scrunch*, *crunch*, and *drip drop*.

A **found poem** is a type of poetry created by taking words and phrases from other sources and reframing them as poetry. Although the words come from other texts, the poet makes changes in spacing and lines to create new meaning. For example, an arrangement of book spines or highlighted words on a page of text can become a poem. A found poem is considered the literary equivalent to a collage.

A **shape poem**, or **concrete poem**, describes an object and the poem also appears in the shape of that object. For example, this poem about a bird "singing sweetly" appears in the shape of a small bird.

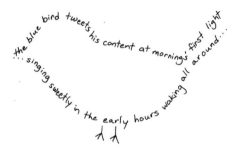

Acrostic is a type of poetry where the first letters in each line spell out a particular word or phrase.

    Loyal
    Optimistic
    Vibrant
    Enduring

Pantoum consists of four-line stanzas in four-stanza, five-stanza, and six-stanza variations. Lines 2 and 4 of each stanza become Lines 1 and 3 of the next stanza. It might sound complicated, but the form kind of writes itself. Here is the pattern for a four-stanza poem:

    1, 2, 3, 4   2, 5, 4, 6   5, 7, 6, 8   7, 1, 8, 3

Free verse is poetry that has no set meter or pattern. It can be rhymed or not rhymed. A good example is "Homework! Oh, Homework!" by Jack Prelutsky.

So much of poetry is the way it sounds and rolls off the tongue. Be sure to teach your students to read their poetry out loud throughout the writing process. Because poetry can be considered a spoken art form, reading the poems aloud will help students find just the right words, hear the cadence of the language, and ensure that their poems have rhythm. It will also help students determine how they want to punctuate their poem to communicate with the reader. Working with their poetry partner or even in their writing groups can help students with this process.

Topic Frames to Further Student Poetry Writing

After you have taught the various forms of poetry, you can motivate students to write more poems by introducing various topics.

- **Color:** For instance, invite students to write a poem about color. Students use a color word at the beginning of each line. Some students use the same color for every line. Others prefer to use a rainbow of colors. Both approaches are effective and the repetition ensures success for all students.
- **Apology:** Challenge students to write an apology poem. Students think of something, real or imagined, that they want to apologize for. The first line could be "I am sorry for …" or "There is something I should tell you." A model apology poem is "This Is Just to Say" by William Carlos Williams.
- **Opposites:** Another idea is for students to write an opposite poem. Alternating lines will begin with contrasting ideas. For example, here are four patterns:

I am …	I lost …	Cats …	Yesterday …
I am not …	I found …	Dogs …	Tomorrow …

- **Objects:** An interesting object can be used to inspire student writing, too: a feather, a key, a baseball glove, a treasure chest, or a teddy bear, for example. Before writing this poem, students simply jot down all the words and ideas that come to them while looking at the object. To provide scaffolding for this brainstorming activity, use a graphic organizer including categories such as a description of the object, uses of the object, or memories that the object evokes. Choose the categories that best fit with the object you have chosen.

As you can see, this week is all about the creation of poems! If needed, extend this one week into two.

Crackling Connections

After your students have had some experience with poetry, challenge them to write a poem about a specific topic in science or social studies. This is an effective way to create enduring learning of a curricular topic and adds a creative element to an often knowledge-based curriculum. Imagine what poems about fractions, magnets, the solar system, democracy, or electricity might result!

Week 3: Revise and Publish

After writing at least 10 to 12 poems over the course of a couple of weeks, the students choose one or two of their favorites (you as teacher can decide how many) to revise, edit, illustrate, and share with their peers.

After the revision process, students spend time planning and creating pictures to accompany one or two of their recent poems. Let them choose how to present their poems: the medium and the layout.

Be open to a variety of mediums and careful not to insist on the same for all students. Students can choose from pastels, chalk, paint, crayons, or collage. If they have access to a computer or an iPad, be open to options such as PowerPoint,

Although most students enjoy the process of illustrating their poems in some way, be aware of students who do not feel comfortable with this process. Encourage these students to use technology to present their poems. Or, they could simply show their attention to the presentation aspect by being very deliberate about the placement of words on their page(s).

Adobe Voice, Animoto, or iMovie. By adding effects, music, and transitions they can enhance and polish the poem before sharing it with others.

As for layout, again, be open. The entire poem could appear on one page. Or, the poem could be illustrated in book form with a line on each page. By your providing choice about the illustrations and presentation, your students will typically take more pride in their work and enjoy the freedom provided.

Time for Sharing

An important and enjoyable culmination to your poetry unit is sharing with an audience. My favorite ways include a poetry reading, a poetry walk, the creation of a class book, and the giving of poems as gifts.

Poetry Reading

In addition to posting poems around the classroom, I plan a poetry reading. Each student chooses one of his or her own poems to read aloud or recite. In preparation, students polish their work and perfect their reading of it.

You can make the reading an event by inviting guests, such as parents, administrators, or another class perhaps. Suggest that students dress a little more formally on this day, too. Bring juice and cookies. Make a schedule so students know in what order they will read. Be sure to include a short intermission.

Poetry Walk

An added touch: play classical music on the school intercom!

If your entire school has been writing poetry at the same time, plan a school-wide poetry walk. Student poems of all grade levels could be posted throughout the school. Students then tour the school, reading the poetry of their peers. Partner younger students with older students to ensure an enjoyable event for all. The older students will have an authentic reading experience as they read aloud the poems to their younger partners; the younger children will love the attention of their older peers. In my fairly large school, the event takes about half an hour.

Class Poetry Book

At the end of the year, you may want to give this treasure to the school library or draw one student's name to determine who will take it home.

Ask your students to print and illustrate one poem they have written on a page you provide. Compile these student poems into a book to include in your classroom library. In my classroom, this book becomes a preferred choice during independent reading time.

Poems as Gifts

Buying frames from the dollar store in advance will let you know what size of paper to give your students for their good copies.

Your students have spent much time writing, revising, and illustrating their poems. Consider framing one poem by each student and having students give their work as a gift for Christmas, Mother's Day, or Father's Day. Since I typically teach my poetry unit in April, framed poetry becomes a timely Mother's Day gift! Students choose the poem they think the recipient would like best.

Literary Conversations

As important as it is to have fun with poetry, it is also important to plan your unit to maximize student learning. You will inevitably have conversations about punctuation, imagery, word choice, and rhythm, but be sure to choose poems to share with students that lend themselves to these literary conversations.

Nancie Atwell (2015) speaks to the myriad of themes that can be included when teaching poetry as a form of writing:

> Every lesson that matters, every essential feature of literature, can be highlighted easily and accessibly in free-verse poems: the need for a writer to find subjects he or she cares about, the importance of first-person voice and reflection, the value of tangible nouns and sensory verbs and adjectives, how to revise and polish and edit, what titles do, why readers want inviting leads and resonant conclusions, how punctuation gives voice to writing, and why and how writers develop and support a theme. (317–18)

As she explains, literary conversations about these matters become timely as students read the poems of others and compose their own poems. The discussion about spacing on the page and the use of punctuation to guide the reader are perhaps most effective and obvious to students when teaching poetry.

A poetry unit is the perfect time to explore figurative language: similes, metaphors, personification, hyperbole, alliteration, and onomatopoeia. For example, when teaching hyperbole, I read the students *Library Lil* by Suzanne Williams and *Finn Throws a Fit!* by David Elliott. Both books use humorous examples of hyperbole which students enjoy emulating in their own writing. An entertaining way to teach the meaning of *alliteration* is by practising tongue twisters. And remember that word *onomatopoeia*? It refers to words that imitate sounds. Some examples: *crack, splat, clunk, woof, bonk, chatter, buzz, crunch, fizz, sizzle, purr, thud,* and *achoo!* Challenge your students to play with the sounds of language and include some examples of onomatopoeia in their own poetry.

By discussing these elements during the poetry unit, students will become much more deliberate in their own word choice, punctuation, and spacing. They will become more attentive readers and notice the author's intentions as well. They will learn to read their work out loud to listen to how it sounds. Some students might even find it helpful to record themselves reading their poems: they can replay the recordings to hear how they sound with a little more perspective.

Poetry can reveal a sense of playfulness in your students and also tug at their heartstrings. Remember, if you take pleasure in this unit, your students will too!

Assessment for Writing and Presentation

I generally ask students to pick two or three poems that they have written for the purpose of assessment. Before they hand in the poems of their choosing, we discuss the rubric so they know what they will be assessed on. Sometimes, the students and I create a rubric together.

Many students (and some adults) assume that poetry must rhyme. In reality, the intent to rhyme can detract from both the process and the product of poetry. The writing may become forced and awkward. You can illustrate this point by using saved student samples of work. Always ask the students for permission to use their work and be sure there is nothing to identify the author.

Poetry Writing Rubric	Exceeds Expectations 5	Meets Expectations 3	Below Expectations 1
Rules of the Poem	Rules of poem were followed completely.	Most rules of poem were followed.	Rules of poem were not followed.
Word Choice	Vivid word choice enhances the poem.	There is some descriptive word choice.	There is limited descriptive word choice.
Conventions	All words are spelled correctly.	There are one or two spelling errors.	There are three or more spelling errors.
Presentation	Presentation is deliberate and interesting. It includes elements such as spacing, punctuation, and illustrations. Poem is neat and easy to read.	Presentation is somewhat deliberate. It includes some elements of spacing, punctuation, and illustrations. Poem is fairly neat and easy to read.	Little or no attention was paid to presentation of poem. Poem is difficult to read.

Poetry Presentation Rubric	Exceeds Expectations 5	Meets Expectations 3	Below Expectations 1
Volume	Poet recites entire poem loudly enough for audience to hear.	Poet recites most of the poem loudly enough for audience to hear.	Poet did not speak loudly enough for audience to hear well.
Inflection and Expression	Poet emphasizes key words and phrases. Poet engages audience fully in poem.	Poet makes some effort to emphasize key words and phrases.	Poet makes no effort to change inflection or use expression.
Posture and Eye Contact	Poet appears confident: stands up straight and makes eye contact with audience at appropriate intervals.	Poet stands up straight and makes eye contact at appropriate intervals during most of the presentation.	Poet fidgets, slouches, or makes no eye contact with audience.
Clarity and Pace	Poet speaks clearly for the entire poem. Pacing is excellent.	Poet speaks clearly for most of the poem. Pacing is good.	Poet mumbles or cannot be understood. Pacing is not effective.

9

Reader Response and Author Studies

"You can't buy happiness but you can buy books and that's kind of the same thing."
— Anonymous

As is evident, I use mentor texts every week of the school year. Sometimes these mentor texts are picture books, sometimes novels, and sometimes selections from an anthology such as *Collections* or *Literacy Place*. We use mentor texts because authors have so much to teach us through their work. One of the most natural forms of writing connected to reading is reader response.

The experiences of a reader can never be entirely anticipated by the author when he or she is composing a text. What's more, those experiences change over time. In my reading of *The Velveteen Rabbit* as an adult, I realized how much we relate literature to our own lives.

> Generally, by the time you are Real, most of your hair has been loved off, and your eyes drop out and you get loose in the joints and very shabby. But these things don't matter at all, because once you are Real you can't be ugly, except to people who don't understand. (Williams 1975, 13)

A writer putting words on paper has an intended meaning; however, each reader brings his or her own life experiences to the reading of the text and therefore the interpretation of the words on the page will differ from person to person.

This description of the velveteen rabbit reminded me of my own father before his death and helped me to come to terms with his illness as his body grew "loose in the joints and very shabby." Margery Williams's story articulates a universal truth just waiting to be discovered, enabling me to make a powerful connection to my own life. "Ultimately … it is the *reader* who interprets the writer," Vivian Paley (1997, 42) writes. Though I loved *The Velveteen Rabbit* as a child, it took on new meaning in my adult years.

Reader Response Writing

What is reader response writing? It is as it sounds: writing down our responses to what we read. Because writing is a form of thinking, reader response writing helps students to engage more fully in what they are reading as a class and what they are reading independently. Teaching students *how* to respond to texts is an important element in reader response. Effective readers naturally make connections to the text they are reading and use their background knowledge to determine whether something makes sense. Struggling readers, on the other hand, often concentrate so hard on each individual word, reading word to word, that

I often use reader response in Kindergarten. After a read-aloud, I provide my Kindergarten students with a blank page and encourage them to *write* about the book. Initially their responses will be exclusively pictures. Eventually they will also begin to include letters and words. When you introduce reader response, be sure to follow the same guidelines as provided for journal entries (see Chapter 5).

they are not able to think about the meaning of text (not to mention, make connections to the text). Keene and Zimmermann (1997) introduced three types of connections that are commonly referred to today: text to self, text to text, and text to world. The rationale behind these types of responses is that we understand more completely when we make connections to our own lives and build on our prior knowledge.

During a Read-Aloud

As I mentioned, I use a scribbler for reader response no matter what grade level I am teaching. If I am reading a novel to my students, Grade 1 through to Grade 6, I encourage my students to have their scribblers open and either draw pictures or write down words and phrases as I am reading.

One way to encourage all students to participate and to set a high standard of quality is to use a gallery walk. After making a reader response entry, students leave their work on their desks and walk quietly around the room, viewing the entries of their peers. It is essential that students are respectful of their classmates' work. The tone is set for this early in the year, but I continually monitor and model my expectations. Students find it interesting to see how differently they respond to the same text being read out loud.

After a Read-Aloud

If I want more of a written reflection on the text read (rather than only pictures and jot notes), I give my students a prompt *after* I finish reading the selection. Students usually complete these reader responses as they would a freewrite based either on a prompt provided or a more open-ended opportunity. Most students will require a prompt to guide their writing, but over the years, I have had some students who had no difficulty responding without a prompt. Ultimately, we want students to make sense of what they have read as well as make connections to the text. As long as they are responding to the text, it doesn't matter if they have used the prompt or not.

Reader Response Prompts

There are several types of effective prompts: questions, sentence prompts, vocabulary prompts, alternative forms of writing, and nonfiction prompts.

Questions

Students can be given specific questions to answer according to the text you've chosen. The more open-ended the questions the better. Be sure to use text to text, text to self, and text to world connections to guide your questioning. Note that some questions are appropriate for the extended reading of a novel and others more appropriate for a single-sitting read-aloud such as a picture book. Choose accordingly. As well, choose the questions or prompts based on the grade level you teach. Not all prompts are appropriate for all ages.

Sample questions:

• Who is your favorite character in the book? Why?

- Why do you think this character did this [specify an event]?
- What would you do if _____ happened to you?
- How are these two characters, _____ and _____, alike? different?
- What do you think will happen next? What are the clues?
- How does this story make you feel?
- Do you think this story could have really happened?
- When and where does this story take place?
- What is the main problem in this story? Who fixes the problem?
- Does this book remind you of anything in your own life?
- Does this book remind you of another book you have read?
- Do any of the characters go through a transformation in this story? What caused the change?
- Do any of the characters remind you of anyone in your own life?
- How do you think the author wants us to feel about the main character?
- Do any of the characters suffer in this story? Who? Why?
- What is your favorite part of this story? Why?
- What is your favorite sentence or phrase in this book?
- Were you surprised by anything in this book?
- Was the ending a good one? Why or why not?

Sometimes, instead of asking questions, prompt your students to write down questions they have about the text. This works especially well for novels that you are reading aloud so students can make predictions about what is to come.

Sentence Prompts

I tend to give my students the choice of two prompts on which to base a reader response. If only one prompt is given, some students may not connect to that particular idea and have more difficulty writing. If two prompts are given, students can choose.

I encourage my students to write their reader responses in the style of a free-write (see Chapter 4). This prevents them from overthinking the prompt and, instead, frees them to write what comes to mind. The purpose is to have students connect with the text, not to produce perfect, precise writing. As always, students can edit and revise later should you decide you want them to.

- This book reminded me of …
- I wish …
- If I could ask the author anything, I would ask …
- I like the way …
- I wonder why …
- I relate to [pick a character] because …
- I would [or wouldn't] recommend this book because …
- I was puzzled by …
- I can't believe …
- I can picture …
- The setting of the story …
- I felt _____ when …

Alternatively, have students pick a sentence from one of the books: something they respond to or connect with in some way. Tell them to write this sentence on the top of a page in their journals and then freewrite about the passage beginning with "I chose this sentence because ..."

Vocabulary Prompts

Another type of prompt focuses on the words the author chose to use. As you can see, these prompts might not yield as much writing as a formal reader response, but they do require higher-level thinking and analysis.

- Find all of the words in today's reading that convey emotion [or food, physical description, setting, the five senses, weather, et cetera].
- Today's reading included these words: _____, _____, and _____. Draw a picture to illustrate the meaning of each word.
- Record the five most interesting words from today's reading or book. Why did you choose these words?
- What words or phrases were used to describe your favorite character?
- What words did you hear or find in today's reading that were new to you? What do you think they mean?
- If you were to define a theme for this book, what would it be? What words can you find in the text to justify this choice of theme?

Prompts for Alternative Forms of Writing

- Write a letter to one of the characters in the book.
- Write a letter to the author.
- Pretend you are one of the characters, and write three journal/diary entries from that point of view.
- Create a timeline of main events in the story.
- Write a text-message conversation between two characters.
- Write three Facebook posts as one of the characters.

Nonfiction Reader Response

Some teachers have expressed the opinion that reader response is something they use for fiction books only; however, reader response can also be effective for nonfiction text, including textbooks.

After reading a nonfiction text, students might work with prompts such as these:

- I learned ...
- I was surprised that ...
- The most interesting thing I discovered ...
- While reading/listening to this book, I felt ...
- This information applies to my own life because ...
- This book reminds me of ...
- The author used these words I had never heard before: _____.
- This book reminded me of another book: _____.
- What was the author's purpose? How did the author meet this purpose?
- What would you change about this book?
- The author used these text features: ...

Author Studies

Although studying individual texts is certainly effective, a powerful way to learn even more from authors is through an author study. Author studies are an effective way for students to improve both their reading and their writing skills. They also often create a deeper attachment to books than children might otherwise have.

For a wonderful read about a Kindergarten class that engages in an author study with the books of Leo Lionni, read *The Girl with the Brown Crayon: How Children Use Stories to Shape Their Lives* by Vivian Gussin Paley.

Make your author selection based on grade level and group dynamics. However, whatever the grade you teach, I would encourage using picture books for this task. Author studies lend themselves to many skills and activities: comparing and contrasting, analyzing texts, persuasion and debate, making connections, and providing authentic writing experiences. All the activities outlined in "Reader Response Writing" and under "Reader Response Prompts" can also be used in an author study.

When choosing which author to study there are a number of things to consider. First, are you choosing the author *for* your students or *with* your students? Either approach will work, but the way the author is introduced is important and can affect the entire author study. If *you* choose the author, be sure to find a way to hook the students. Second, will all students study the same author, or will you create smaller groups that can each study a different author? Again, both methods are effective, but consider the dynamics of your class. What will be most effective for your group of students?

An author study typically creates a connection between students and author, even a love for the author. Students are often surprised at how many books are written by the same author. Through their experience of an author study, they come to learn that when they enjoy a book, they should look for other books by that author. They will likely enjoy those books too!

As you prepare for the author study gather a collection of as many titles as possible. Draw from your own collection of books, access the public library and your school library, borrow from colleagues, and even check to see if your school district has a collection. The more books that are accessible in your classroom during the author study, the more options you and your students will have!

Effective Authors for an Author Study

I have selected a few favorite authors for you to consider. You will notice that some of the authors are on both the Kindergarten to Grade 3 and Grades 4 to 6 lists. That is because they write for various age groups; choose the books most appropriate for your level of students. However, if you teach students in Grades 4 to 6, don't shy away from sharing the books written by your author that might be geared more for a primary audience. Including them shows the whole scope of the author and helps students to better understand the author's style and interests. The same is true for the primary students to a certain extent.

Picture Books, Kindergarten to Grade 3	Picture Books, Grades 4 to 6
Mac Barnett Jan Brett Eric Carle Doreen Cronin Tomie de Paola Lois Ehlert Douglas Florian Mem Fox Phoebe Gilman Kevin Henkes Oliver Jeffers Steve Jenkins Ezra Jack Keats Leo Lionni Arnold Lobel Bill Martin Jr. Robert Munsch Laura Numeroff Patricia Polacco Peter H. Reynolds Cynthia Rylant Dr. Seuss David Shannon Chris Van Allsburg Mélanie Watt Rosemary Wells Mo Willems	Jan Brett Eve Bunting Janell Cannon Tomie de Paola Oliver Jeffers Steve Jenkins Ezra Jack Keats David Macaulay Kathryn Otoshi Patricia Polacco Peter H. Reynolds Cynthia Rylant Jon Scieszka Maurice Sendak William Steig Chris Van Allsburg Mélanie Watt
	Middle Readers/Novels, Grades 4 to 6
	Katherine Applegate Judy Blume Betsy Byars Kate DiCamillo Carl Hiaasen Gordon Korman Jerry Spinelli Eric Wilson

Determining What Students Know and Want to Find Out

Author Websites

More and more authors are directing their websites to children. In addition, many authors of children's books include a teacher section on their websites. An author website is the first place to check once your author is chosen. Steve Jenkins has one of my favorite author websites for children. The site has a section on making books and how he finds his inspiration: perfect for an author study!

Begin the author study by asking your students if they know any books by the author you have selected. Generate a list of the books that your students are familiar with. Then, together, research other books by the same author. Involve students in the process (even though you have likely already accessed titles and have them ready to show).

Together with your students, generate a list of questions to ask about this author and his or her books: questions that you as a class want to explore.

- How are the books of this author alike? How are they different?
- What is the style of this author?
- What types of books does this author like to write?
- How does this author choose topics and themes?

If you have chosen a novelist, such as one of the strong ones included on my list above, I suggest beginning the author study earlier in the year and preparing to devote more time to it. Nonetheless, my preference remains picture books for this purpose.

A Way to Promote Response and Skills

Journalling on a regular basis is recommended throughout an author study.

Ask students to journal in the style of a reader response throughout the author study. I like to have students use a new scribbler dedicated to this purpose. Within this journal, students could record facts they discover, freewrite about what they learn, create Venn diagrams, and even respond visually to the author's texts. Some students may prefer more open-ended opportunities while others will always need a prompt. Allow for this flexibility. Choose one or two reader response prompts from the beginning of this chapter for each journalling session. There are two questions I often return to during an author study:

1. How does this book make you feel?
2. What does this book remind you of?

Compare and Contrast

An author study is the perfect opportunity to introduce or reinforce the idea of a Venn diagram for students at any grade level. Model the creation of a Venn diagram using two of the author's books you have already read. Then, either in small groups or on their own, students choose a topic on which to create their own Venn diagram. Venn diagrams can be used to compare two books by the same author, two characters within a book, a character and the student, the author study author and another author, or the setting in the book and the students' own environment — the possibilities are endless. Students can create their Venn diagrams either in their author study scribblers or in their visual journals.

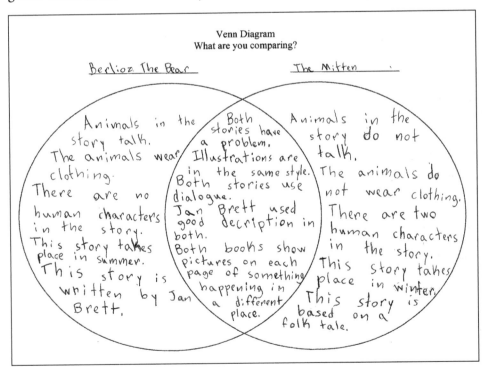

This student-created Venn diagram compares two picture books by Jan Brett, Berlioz the Bear *and* The Mitten.

Analyze Texts

My students and I create a display of all of the books by the author. On one side of the shelf we display the books we have already read; on the other side of the shelf are the ones we have yet to read. This is a simple but effective visual for the students. And, if they happen to pull one of the books off the shelf for independent reading time, wonderful: they have no difficulty remembering where to put it afterwards. As you proceed through the unit and read more books by your chosen author, take the opportunity to analyze not only the individual books but also the group of texts.

An author study gives students a reason to analyze the texts you are reading. During and after reading, consider these questions for discussion. Some are appropriate for fiction, some are appropriate for nonfiction, and some are effective for both.

For individual texts, consider these questions for discussion:

- How do the text and pictures work together?
- What emotion is conveyed by the author? How is this emotion created?
- What do you notice about the author's choice of words?
- What do you notice about the author's sentence length?
- Does this author use dialogue? To what effect?
- Does this author create a strong sense of setting? If so, how?
- Are there any tough questions or big ideas explored in this book?
- Which character do you relate to? Why? How are you the same?
- What does this book remind you of?

For the group of texts, consider these questions for discussion:

- Is there a common theme among the books by this author?
- Does the author write fiction, nonfiction, or both?
- What text features does this author like to use?
- What is the author's purpose in writing? To entertain? To teach something?
- What can we infer about the author from the group of books gathered? (Examples: interests, personality)
- Does this author like to use any literary tools such as alliteration, rhythm, rhyme, repetition, or personification? What are some examples?
- Do any of the author's books follow any of the plot patterns that we have studied? (See Chapter 6.)
- Do characters overlap from one book to another?
- Is this author also the illustrator of any of his/her books?

Persuade and Debate

One of my favorite activities near the end of an author study is to have students write about their favorite book by this author. To push it into a higher level of thinking the assignment could be, "why everyone in our school/class should read this book." The assignment can begin as a freewrite and then be edited, revised, and discussed within writing groups to improve the work. Remind students of the elements of opinion pieces and persuasive writing taught earlier in the year.

Gather the students for a debate about their favorite book by your featured author. Students enjoy persuading others, and the discussion often becomes quite passionate. I always give my students more time to revise their work after the debate because ideas often surface during the debate itself.

After the writing has been polished, create a bulletin board to feature it. This bulletin board becomes a fascinating compilation of the author's work according to student favorites. Be sure to keep this work up for the upcoming author party!

Connect with the Author

Students may enjoy writing to the author, if living. Many authors welcome this correspondence. (Check the author website for details.) Students can write individual letters or the class could write one letter together. A local author could be invited to your classroom. If the author is in a different locale, though, you could invite the author to Skype with your class.

Help the students make connections between the author's life and the books written by ordering the books by date published. I give a book and a sticky note to students working as partners. I teach the students to find the publication date and they write it on the sticky note and place it on the front of the book. Then, as a class we make a timeline by ordering the books from earliest to most recent. One student from each pair stands holding their book with the year on the front until we have all of the books ordered. We then analyze the books according to the timeline. Are there patterns? themes? If the author wrote a series of books, were they written consecutively?

Create Pictorial Responses to Texts

Near the end of the unit, ask students to create a pictorial response to one book or the collection of books by the author you are studying. Give students ample time to create this response in their visual journals. They can use a combination of pictures and words and a variety of mediums. This creative opportunity often leads to meaningful, profound connections. Once the visual responses are complete be sure to give an opportunity for students to travel from desk to desk for a gallery walk.

Final Project

Be open to the use of many kinds of formats, such as letters, speeches, advertisements (posters, commercials), book trailers, presentations, book reviews, and display boards.

For a culminating project, let students pick one of the following assignments.

- Develop a timeline display of the author's work.
- Create a game of trivia about the author.
- Dramatize one of the author's books.
- Create a display board featuring the life and books of the author.
- Write a collection of poems about the author and his/her books.
- Write and perform a song related to the author or any of the books read.
- Develop an award to present to the author. What award is it? Why is the author deserving of this award?

As students are working, I meet briefly with each individual to discuss what he or she has decided to create and how it will be carried out. I record a quick note about each of their project plans so that I can check in and follow up as necessary.

Plan to give students class time to work on their projects. I find an hour each day over two or three days is usually enough, but judge the time needed according to your group of students and the projects they have chosen. Begin this working time by asking students to meet in their writing groups to discuss ideas. You could even have them check in with their writing groups at the beginning of each day's project time to discuss their progress and potential obstacles.

Author Party

Organize an author party where your students' culminating projects will be showcased. Students who have created visual or written projects can display them. Students who have prepared a presentation or speech may present it to the guests. To help create a sense of occasion, you might draw up a guest list and invite parents or another class to the event.

Depending on who the author is, you could choose a theme for the party. For example, if your class has been studying Steve Jenkins, most of whose books are nonfiction titles about animals, the theme of your party could pertain to animals. The invitations might say, "Join us in our zoo!" and feature torn-paper collage animals to mimic the way Jenkins illustrates many of his books. The refreshments served could also be related to the author or a favorite character, but cookies and juice are common. These simple details become very motivating for the students.

Assessment for an Author Study

There is no need to assess every task or activity within an author study. Typically during the unit, I assess a Venn diagram and the persuasive writing piece that features the student's favorite book. I also consider the effort put into the pictorial response and the regular reader responses: I do not assess the content of either of these.

For certain, the culminating project should be assessed. For best results create a rubric together as a class, deciding on elements that you expect to see in all final projects.

10
Teaching Skills

Stephen King is the author of more than 60 books and nearly 200 short stories. His books have reportedly sold over 350 million copies. If Stephen King's advice to writers is to read, then I think we should listen!

Writing is not only about the finished product: it is about the process. If we, as teachers, see writing as a process — a valuable and necessary process — so, too, will our students. This mindset requires a shift for many teachers who have reasonably believed that their focus on mechanics and grammar in their students' good copies was most important. As we shift to understand that writing is about conveying meaning (and that all of us want to convey meaning to others), we begin to see how the process of selecting appropriate language, as well as manipulating that language until it is just right, is an essential part of writing.

Students will become more invested in the process of writing if we convince them that what they have to say is important. When we stress less about mechanics and, instead, show genuine interest in what they say, students will begin to care about what they write. What happens then is a willingness to revise and edit. Students even become excited about engaging in this process because they want to make their writing the best it can be. When students begin to invest in their writing, they want to learn how to make it more effective.

Therefore, writing alone is not enough: ongoing literary conversations are necessary. Students need effective instruction, exemplars, and scaffolding if their writing is going to show significant improvement. The literary conversations in my classroom stem from mini-lessons that always include mentor texts and guided writing.

Mini-lessons

Most mini-lessons include the use of mentor texts and guided writing.

At least once a week, I teach mini-lessons specific to skills and techniques involved in the writing process. I do not plan my mini-lessons in advance of the year; I respond to the needs of the group of writers before me. Often however, based on my overall year plan, I find certain skills tend to surface at similar times during the year while we are exploring particular genres. For instance, the need to teach dialogue will likely surface during the teaching of narrative writing and not before. Although I still work my way through the curriculum, the reading within the classroom and the needs of the students become the inspiration and impetus for my mini-lessons.

I teach some skills as mini-lessons to the whole class of students: skills that all students could benefit from. There are other skills I teach as mini-lessons only to part of the class: something applicable only to a small group of students. For instance, if a few students were struggling with inserting basic punctuation, I might pull only them aside; it would be a waste of time for the others. Let the majority continue with their writing while you target a small group with timely instruction.

In order to ensure student engagement during mini-lessons, keep the lessons fairly short. As with anything, the longer you talk, the less interest there will be from the class. Engage as many of your students as possible in the process by continually asking for student ideas and input. Consider giving students a specific purpose during the lesson, for example: "Find one thing that you could do to improve your writing based on our guided writing experience today." Or, ask them to consider a question, such as "How can you use the techniques we are discussing today to assist the others in your writing group?"

Another strategy that works well to ensure student engagement is having students meet in their writing groups before your mini-lesson. Let's say you have been working on writing news articles. Students in writing groups could share the articles they have written before your lesson. Then, during the mini-lesson, you could encourage students to think about how the skills and strategies will help improve both their own articles and those of their peers. The writing will be fresh in their minds.

To ensure that a mini-lesson experience is effective and useful for students, I sometimes provide a *prompt page* for students to record their thoughts during or after the lesson. For example:

What did you learn about the structure of an article from today's lesson?

What are you going to do to improve the structure of your article?

Notice that the questions are specific and require students to first summarize what they've learned and then apply it to their own work. This is the format I would use with any topic.

I do not use prompt pages every time I teach a mini-lesson, but I do use them often enough that they hold my students accountable and encourage literate thinking.

Mentor Texts

As in other chapters, I have included a list of mentor texts for various skills. Keep in mind, though, if I have suggested one book by an author as a mentor text, very likely his or her other books would make excellent mentor texts, as well.

My preference is to use a mentor text for almost every skill I teach. Why? We can learn from the writing of professionals by examining quality literature. When choosing a mentor text, I look for one that highlights a skill connected to what I've noticed in my students' writing. Perhaps the writer of a particular mentor text uses words or images that evoke emotion. That day we might focus on word choice in our own writing. Perhaps the writer uses a variety of sentence lengths and structures. As writers ourselves, we might attempt to vary our sentence lengths and structures to improve the impact of our work. Obviously, the timelier the lesson for the students, the better.

Guided Writing

The use of guided writing is essential for students to solidify their understanding of the concept you are teaching during a mini-lesson. It is an effective way to demonstrate a skill either for the whole class or for a smaller group of students. As Vicki Spandel (2001) suggests, one benefit of writing in front of your students is this: "Students mostly see finished pieces of writing. Rarely do they have a chance to see a writer drafting, pausing, crossing out, rewriting, stopping to think, or asking for help" (239). As we talk through the writing that we are completing together, students will learn strategies that they can use when writing independently. I use guided writing with every form of writing I teach.

I recognize that some teachers are hesitant to write in front of their class. As Regie Routman (2014) says: "Even if you are reluctant and fearful to publicly write, give it a sincere attempt. Students appreciate honest efforts. Not only that, but thinking out loud and writing in front of our students is the number one strategy for improving students' writing" (112).

We can use guided writing to demonstrate different stages of the writing process. As we compose a letter, an article, or the beginning of a narrative as a class, for example, the process of drafting is demonstrated. Sometimes, I use guided writing to demonstrate the revision process as we change our sentence structure, reorganize our paragraphs, or add more interesting vocabulary. Regardless of the purpose of the lesson, guided writing provides teachers with the opportunity to talk through their thought processes and model effective writing.

Notes on Assessment

Assessment is a critical component in the teaching of all writing skills. As part of your mini-lessons, students should have the opportunity to explore and discuss the rubric or standards for each of the skills you are teaching. Only then can they strive to improve their work through self-assessment, discussion in writing groups, and revision.

To save on time, consider assessing only the skill you have been focusing on within your student writing.

What Skills to Teach

We have discussed *how* to teach skills, but now we will delve into *what* to teach. The previous chapters addressed skills specific to a genre of writing. The remainder of this chapter will focus on skills or processes that are applicable to all genres: ideas and content, organization, voice, word choice, sentence fluency, revision, and editing (including the teaching of conventions).

Ideas and Content

Effective Mentor Texts	Ideas and Content
Grades 1 to 2	*All the Places to Love* by Patricia MacLachlan *And to Think That I Saw It on Mulberry Street* by Dr. Seuss *David's Drawings* by Cathryn Falwell *Fireflies!* by Julie Brinckloe *J. Rooker, Manatee* by Jan Haley *Something Beautiful* by Sharon Dennis Wyeth *Tuesday* by David Wiesner
Grades 3 to 6	*All the Places to Love* by Patricia MacLachlan *The Best Story* by Eileen Spinelli *Creepy Creatures* by Sneed B. Collard III *J. Rooker, Manatee* by Jan Haley *Nothing Ever Happens on 90th Street* by Roni Schotter *The Other Side* by Jacqueline Woodson *Something Beautiful* by Sharon Dennis Wyeth *Tuesday* by David Wiesner *What Do You Do with an Idea?* by Kobi Yamada *What Do You Do with a Problem?* by Kobi Yamada *Wilfrid Gordon McDonald Partridge* by Mem Fox

When teaching the concept of ideas and content, focus on three main components: writing with (1) detail, (2) relevance, and (3) clarity.

Writing with Detail

Begin by helping students to identify interesting details in the texts you are reading. Read aloud examples of detail from one of the mentor texts suggested. Good details in fiction often create effective imagery, character development, or a clear, engaging story. *All the Places to Love* by Patricia MacLachlan is my favorite mentor text for this discussion. Effective details in nonfiction often include something unexpected or unusual. Use any National Geographic or Usborne book for children as a mentor text for this discussion.

After my students hear a few examples of effective detail, I give them tiny Post-it notes to flag interesting details as they search through the books in our classroom, fiction or nonfiction. They can present a passage and explain why they think the detail is effective. This is also the time to discuss how much information or detail an author chose to include and why.

Writing with Relevance

The second key component of ideas and content is staying on topic: relevance. Especially when freewriting, students may include a variety of topics within their writing. As you model the revision process and conference with students, they begin to understand how to narrow their focus to one main topic and delete anything unneeded or irrelevant. Freewriting thus becomes the means by which students tend to grasp this concept best; however, with practice, they will be able to translate the skill of maintaining focus into their other forms of writing.

Writing with Clarity

The third component of ideas and content is clarity. I spend considerable time teaching my students to summarize what they read: fiction and nonfiction alike. The more practice students have in summarizing texts, and the more discussion you have about clarity in an author's writing, the better they will be able to identify how to create clarity in their own writing. Consider these questions: Is the author's message clear? What does the author do to achieve this clarity? After students have had practice summarizing another author's work, ask them to summarize their own piece of writing. If they cannot do this with ease, likely their work lacks clarity.

How Teaching Focus Differs with Genre

The specific teaching of ideas and content varies depending on the genre.

When writing narrative stories, plot patterns assist considerably with ideas and content. The structure of a beginning, middle, and end is inherent in the plot pattern. The challenge is sometimes to ensure that students have included enough detail and information within each of these sections. This is where conferencing and mini-lessons are useful.

When my students are writing transactional pieces, I focus on helping them to consider the audience. *What does the audience want or need to know?* By my posing this question, students write and revise with the audience in mind, striving to include both detailed and relevant information. The structure of the particular piece will also help to ensure clarity.

Organization

Effective Mentor Texts	Organization
Grades 1 to 2	*Alexander and the Terrible, Horrible, No Good, Very Bad Day* by Judith Viorst *Click, Clack, Moo: Cows That Type* by Doreen Cronin *How to Catch a Star* by Oliver Jeffers *The Very Hungry Caterpillar* by Eric Carle *Wild* by Emily Hughes
Grades 3 to 6	*Alexander and the Terrible, Horrible, No Good, Very Bad Day* by Judith Viorst *Sam and Dave Dig a Hole* by Mac Barnett *Scaredy Squirrel* by Mélanie Watt *Smoky Night* by Eve Bunting *The Whales' Song* by Dyan Sheldon

What drives the teaching of organization? Without it, our writing is scattered and confused.

To help students understand organization within writing, I equate it to classroom organization. I have even gone so far as to put on a little act for my students: I make sure that my desk is especially messy, I can't find what I need, I am unprepared for the lesson, and my lesson is confusing for the students. I might even ask them to complete an assignment but not give them any of the required information. Because they know me, they know something is up. Eventually, I ask students to tell me what was wrong with my lesson. Sometimes, the word *disorganized* will surface during the discussion. But even if it doesn't, the students' description of what occurred defines the concept.

I then transfer the discussion to writing. I ask the students what disorganization looks like in writing. Talking about organization becomes easier when we understand *dis*organization. As my students tell me, organization in writing means there is some sort of structure, things make sense, the audience can follow what is being said, and information is complete and contributing to the topic.

The most important thing to remember when helping students organize their writing is to provide some sort of structure. Narrative writing uses plot patterns. Letter writing requires an opening, body, and closing. Both opinion and persuasion pieces include the opening (which states an opinion), the body (which presents reasons and evidence), and the closing (where the argument is wrapped up). Article writing uses the inverted pyramid. Even most of the poetry I teach provides students with a particular form to follow. When we teach these structures, our students will become more adept writers who recognize structure and more habitually use it within their writing.

An important concept in the teaching of organization is that of effective transitions. Students need to understand how an author moves from one idea to the next. Search for transition words in the texts you are reading. Then, generate a list of transitional words with students. Although the list is endless, I focus on the more common ones with students: *first, second, then, next, after, eventually, all of a sudden, for example, such as, equally important, in contrast, in summary, finally.* Each year, depending on what grade I am teaching, my students and I create a poster of transition words. Sometimes our discussion leads to a categorization of the words. Ideas for categorizations include fiction, nonfiction, time, sequencing, adding, comparing, and contrasting.

Although the teaching of organization can mean different things in different genres, once students understand organization and structure in one genre, with a little guidance their understanding transfers over to other forms of writing.

If you are teaching organization in a traditional narrative, the mentor texts for plot patterns are a good start (see Chapter 6). The books on the Organization list here give another structure to follow. For example, in *Click, Clack, Moo: Cows That Type*, the problem is clearly presented at the beginning of the story and then the narrative is driven back and forth through notes between the animals and the farmer. For another example, students can explore *Scaredy Squirrel*. The authors of these books, Doreen Cronin and Mélanie Watt, had a very clear organizational structure in mind when writing. I also like using *The Very Hungry Caterpillar* because the story is organized by the days of the week: "On Monday ..." The more texts the students discuss and explore for organization, the more options they will have within their own writing.

Where Structure Matters Less

There are two exceptions where I deliberately provide less structure: journal writing (where I encourage the writing to be more open-ended and student driven) and freewriting (where we are initially encouraging a free flow of ideas). It is also important to realize that although an inherent structure benefits most students, you may be privileged to encounter a few students whose creativity blossoms with freedom. Respect and celebrate the talent of these individuals.

Voice

Effective Mentor Texts	Voice
Grades 1 to 6	*A Bad Case of Stripes* by David Shannon *Alexander and the Terrible, Horrible, No Good, Very Bad Day* by Judith Viorst *Amazing Grace* by Mary Hoffman *Click, Clack, Moo: Cows That Type* by Doreen Cronin *Dear Mrs. LaRue: Letters from Obedience School* by Mark Teague *I Want My Hat Back* by Jon Klassen *The Magic Hat* by Mem Fox *Nettie's Trip South* by Ann Turner *Owl Moon* by Jane Yolen *Sleeping Ugly* by Jane Yolen *Thank You, Mr. Falker* by Patricia Polacco *Tough Cookie* by David Wisniewski *The True Story of the Three Little Pigs* by Jon Scieszka *Verdi* by Janell Cannon *When I Was Young in the Mountains* by Cynthia Rylant

One of the elements found in effective writing is *voice*. Voice tends to be more difficult to explain and teach as compared to the other traits. "The term has been used in such a loose and celebratory way as to mean almost anything. It's become a kind of warm fuzzy word ... We're in trouble if we don't know what we mean by the term" (Elbow 1994, 2). When I read a piece with strong voice, I can recognize it, as can most teachers. A lack of voice is also easily recognizable. However, how do we help our students to identify voice or the lack thereof in what they read? How do we teach them to develop their own voice?

To begin, we must help students to understand what voice means. Just as those who know us recognize our speaking voice — our inflections, tone, intonation, volume, and even our diction choices — our writing, too, should have a strong voice which enables the reader to recognize that profoundly human and authentic part of us.

> Voice is what allows the reader's eyes to move over silent print and hear the writer speaking. Voice is the quality in writing, more than any other, that makes the reader read on, that makes the reader interested in what is being said and makes the reader trust the person who is saying it. (Murray 2004, 195)

I Want My Hat Back by Jon Klassen and The Magic Hat by Mem Fox make another good pairing to compare voice. The two short picture books can easily be read in the same sitting. The discussion about voice becomes especially effective because both books are about a hat.

As with the other traits, we begin our teaching of voice through the reading of mentor texts. I begin by using two mentor texts with contrasting voices: *Dear Mrs. LaRue: Letters from Obedience School* by Mark Teague and *Owl Moon* by Jane Yolen. In the first, Ike (a dog who has been sent to obedience school) is desperate and unhappy. Students can easily identify sentences with strong voice such as "How could you do this to me? This is a PRISON, not a school!" In contrast, the little girl's voice in *Owl Moon* is calm and subdued: "But I never called out. If you go owling you have to be quiet, that's what Pa always says. I had been waiting to go owling with Pa for a long, long time." The more we read with our students, the more we talk about voice, the better our students will understand what it is and how to ensure its presence in their own writing.

Many young children seem to have a natural voice when they begin writing. "Unskilled writers who are not worried — usually unschooled writers — tend to write prose that is very audible and speech-like" (Elbow 1994, 8). As students get older, they seem to develop a sense of apprehension and self-consciousness about their writing. "It's their worry about conforming to our particular conventions of writing and their fear of mistakes" (Elbow 1994, 8). Do students *lose* their voices, then, as they begin to worry about how their writing will be perceived or worse, marked up with red pen? How do we teach our students to overcome this self-consciousness or fear that many develop?

As discussed in Chapter 4, the practice of *freewriting* typically helps students to write more freely without concern about an audience or final product. They know their freewriting is a first draft only. They know they can make changes later. They also know they can decide whether to share this particular piece of writing or not. These qualities of freewriting, then, enable students to write without a lot of worry or fear.

Interestingly enough, students often *do* want to share this writing because they tend to be impressed with what they have written during a freewrite. I can confirm that for my students and for myself, the voice in a freewrite is often stronger — especially the longer we write. Here, the writing is raw, from the heart. And then, when we spend time revising, our writing voice is strengthened and gains even more personality and power. During freewriting, the hope is that we dive into our subject without pause; the revision process then allows us to reflect on what we have written and strengthen our voice even further.

Letter writing is another excellent way of teaching voice to our students. When writing a letter, we have an audience in mind. Asking students to write two letters one after the other, one to their grandmother and one to the mayor, for example, could help students identify and explore different voices within their writing. As students begin to recognize their voices within their own writing, the presence of voice will begin to transfer to all genres.

The more we read with our students, the more they will understand that strong writers have strong voice. To nurture a strong voice in our writers, we must maintain an environment that allows our students to take risks in their writing, thereby discovering their voices and gaining confidence to reveal those voices to an audience.

Word Choice

Effective Mentor Texts	Word Choice
Grades 1 to 2	*The Bear and the Piano* by David Litchfield *Canoe Days* by Gary Paulsen *Dear Deer: A Book of Homophones* by Gene Barretta *Fancy Nancy's Favorite Fancy Words* by Jane O'Connor *The Loud Book!* by Deborah Underwood *Over and under the Snow* by Kate Messner *The Quiet Book* by Deborah Underwood *The Snowy Day* by Ezra Jack Keats (onomatopoeia) *This House, Once* by Deborah Freedman *Too Much Noise* by Ann McGovern

Grades 3 to 6	*The Bear and the Piano* by David Litchfield*
	Come on, Rain! by Karen Hesse
	Crickwing by Janelle Cannon
	Dear Deer: A Book of Homophones by Gene Barretta*
	Duke Ellington: The Piano Prince and His Orchestra by
	Andrea Davis Pinkney
* Even though these	*Fancy Nancy's Favorite Fancy Words* by Jane O'Connor*
texts are for younger	*A Symphony of Whales* by Steve Schuch
students, they are ideal	*This House, Once* by Deborah Freedman*
for introducing the	*Thunder Cake* by Patricia Polacco (onomatopoeia)
corresponding concepts.	*Tough Boris* by Mem Fox

One of the best ways to improve your students' vocabulary is by reading to them. Whatever their age, they will be introduced to new words through the books you read. Within word choice, we can focus on everything from adjectives to alliteration, strong verbs to sensory language, dialogue tags to figurative language. Although I have suggested a variety of books for word choice, become accustomed to paying closer attention to the choice of words in the books you are reading to your students. When you pay closer attention, so, too, will your students.

Making Lists

Whatever you choose to focus on, make an anchor chart with your students. Do not place a poster of interesting words on the wall that the students have had no part in creating. It will rarely be referenced. Instead, create lists with your students. If you are concentrating on dialogue tags, together with your students make a list titled *Instead of Said*. Use a mentor text to begin your list. Then, in upcoming days, weeks, and months, the students will add to the list as they come across an interesting word. The ongoing attention to this list (and others) will remind students to refer to the lists when they are writing.

These are the list titles I have used with my students:

- *Instead of Said* (dialogue tags)
- *Went Is Spent* (words instead of *went*)
- *Fancy Words* (inspired by *Fancy Nancy's Favorite Fancy Words*)
- *Simply Buzzing* (onomatopoeia — words that imitate sounds)
- *I, Eye!* (homophones) (See the list below.)

I begin each of these lists at different times of the year depending on our current curricular focus.

As mentioned in Chapter 6, if you decide to teach your students to use words other than *said*, also teach them that they should not avoid the word *said* altogether. Too many alternatives can detract from the overall readability of the text.

Sometimes we shy away from more difficult words with our students. And yet, I have discovered that in most classrooms, there are students who will gobble up those difficult words, adopt them in their own speech, and eventually apply them to their own writing. After all, if they don't hear more difficult words, how will they ever improve their vocabulary?

Sentence Fluency

Effective Mentor Texts	Sentence Fluency
Grades 1 to 2	*All the Places to Love* by Patricia MacLachlan *The Bear and the Piano* by David Litchfield *Frederick* by Leo Lionni *Owl Moon* by Jane Yolen *The Snowy Day* by Ezra Jack Keats *Water Dance* by Thomas Locker
Grades 3 to 6	*The Bear and the Piano* by David Litchfield *Goal!* by Mina Javaherbin *Ish* by Peter H. Reynolds *It Takes a Village* by Jane Cowen-Fletcher *My Man Blue* by Nikki Grimes *Owl Moon* by Jane Yolen *Possum Magic* by Mem Fox *Something from Nothing* by Phoebe Gilman *The Whales' Song* by Dyan Sheldon *Tough Boris* by Mem Fox *Water Dance* by Thomas Locker

When teaching sentence fluency, discuss sentence length, sentence beginnings, sentence structure, and the rhythm and sound of sentences. As Ruth Culham (2003) suggests, "To develop an acuity for fluency, student writers must use both their eyes and their ears as they write" (196).

The mentor texts referenced tend to have a wide variety of sentences within their pages. Students need to be taught that varied sentences are used deliberately and not by coincidence. For instance, in *Frederick*, Leo Lionni wrote:

> But the farmers had moved away, the barn was abandoned, and the granary stood empty. And since winter was not far off, the little mice began to gather corn and nuts and wheat and straw. They all worked day and night. All — except Frederick.

There are many things to highlight from this page of text. The first thing I would ask the students to notice is the length of sentences. The first two are fairly long, the third sentence significantly shorter, and the final sentence quite short. That final sentence, deliberately short and structured with an em dash, emphasizes the difference between Frederick and the other mice.

The next thing I would talk about is the structure of each sentence. The first is a list of three events separated by commas. The second sentence is cause (*And since winter was not far off*) and effect (*the little mice began to gather corn and nuts and wheat and straw*). The third sentence contains a simple structure of a subject (*They all*: the mice) and a predicate (*worked day and night*). And as already discussed, the final sentence is intentionally short with use of an em dash to add emphasis. Point out the word *all* in both the third and fourth sentences. How would the sentences change without that word? This is a good time to discuss how sentences sound: the word *all* is purposeful repetition and also adds an effective rhythm to the page of text.

Another effective lesson on sentence fluency focuses on the story *Something from Nothing* by Phoebe Gilman. Not only are the individual sentences crafted with beautiful rhythm, but the repetition of sentences and sentence patterns from page to page make this book an excellent teaching tool.

> One day his mother said to him, "Joseph, look at your blanket. It's frazzled, it's worn, it's unsightly, it's torn. It is time to throw it out."
> "Grandpa can fix it," Joseph said.
> Joseph's grandfather took the blanket and turned it round and round. "Hmm," he said as his scissors went snip, snip, snip and his needle flew in and out and in and out. "There's just enough material here to make ..."
> ... a wonderful jacket. Joseph put on the wonderful jacket and went outside to play.
> But as Joseph grew older, the wonderful jacket grew older too.

This segment of text runs four pages and is repeated with slight variations as the story progresses. The repetition of phrases creates an engaging and endearing read for children of all ages. We can certainly learn from it as writers!

Sentence fluency is not something most students pay attention to unless we direct them to do so. However, by studying sentences together as a class and by mimicking the sentences through guided writing, students will become much more deliberate in their sentence lengths and structure when writing independently. Best of all, they will begin to listen to how a sentence sounds and know whether or not it works.

As you read aloud to your class, consider what you could discuss about the sentences in the books you are reading. You will not want to discuss sentence fluency (or any trait) every time you read a story, but be on the lookout for effective examples!

Revision: A Liberating Process

As teachers, we have to give our young writers motivation to revise. For some students and even some adults, *revision* is a foul word. And yet we can empower our students by showing them that revision is a writer's greatest friend. When we taught students how to freewrite, we told them not to worry about spelling, organization, punctuation, or anything else during the writing. It is later that we go back and look at our work and decide how to make it stronger.

Revision is a frame of mind. Just as the process of freewriting can be liberating, so, too, is the process of revision. The understanding that we can later revise our work enables the initial writing to be much less threatening. For revision to be most effective, I prefer that it not occur on the same day as the initial writing. By giving our students choice in what they revise, they are typically choosing something they wrote on a previous day anyhow. Calkins (2006) states, "Revision means, quite literally, to see again" (12). In my experience, we *see again* most effectively with some time and distance from our work.

Demonstrate the Process

Many students simply do not understand what it means to revise. For this reason, I model the revision process using something I have written. I find it especially effective to use a freewrite for this purpose. Perhaps not all of my writing was on the same topic: I show students how I cross out sentences, sometimes even a whole paragraph. I also add a word, phrase, or sentence to show them how to expand and improve my work. I change any uninteresting word to a more interesting one. I might combine two or three sentences into one. Or, perhaps I move a sentence into another place in the paragraph. All of these demonstrations show students how writing can be significantly improved with a bit of time after the initial writing session.

There is no need to demonstrate all of these revisions at once. You will model the revision process many times, and eventually, you will model each of these techniques. As you revise, be sure to read the work — the possible revisions — out loud several times. This strategy is invaluable during the revision process in order to determine what works and sounds best.

In addition to using freewrites, you can use samples you invent. For example: "We got a new dog yesterday. It is a cocker spaniel. He is brown. He is cute." With a little bit of revision, demonstrated with the students, the sentence can become, "Yesterday, we adopted an adorable cocker spaniel! He's the color of cocoa." By your illustrating the difference between drafts, students begin to understand how empowering revision can be. Something they considered boring or poorly written initially can be the starting point for something greater. This understanding also reinforces the idea that their initial writing does not have to be perfect or dazzling.

Ensure Feedback and Focused Teaching

Hard Copy Revision

If you have taught your students to double-space their writing, revision can be done effectively right on the page. For example, I encourage my students to cross out words and insert their more effective choices above the previous ones. This way, we — teacher and students — can see the changes that are made. The use of highlighters and Post-it notes can also be helpful. Sometimes, I will ask students to highlight or flag a particular element within their own writing: text features, dialogue tags, or fancy words, for instance. These hard-copy revisions reveal how much or how little a student is engaging in the revision process and can help guide our lessons.

Often, I invite students to engage in the revision process after they have met with their writing groups. I will direct the writing groups to discuss a particular element of their work. Perhaps the class has been focusing on using a variety of sentence lengths and structures: the discussion in the groups that day would focus directly on that element of their work. After hearing feedback from their peers, students then return to their desks more focused and excited about revising.

Depending on the genre of text students are revising, you can create mini-lessons directed at improving their work. If students are focusing on narrative writing, you can teach them how to insert dialogue effectively or add descriptive words to improve their development of the character or setting. If students are working on a freewrite, you can teach them how to revise for a more effective beginning or for improved organization. If students are writing letters, you can model effective paragraphing. Gear your revision mini-lessons to something timely for your students.

Cut, Cut, Cut

One of my favorite tricks of revision for my own writing is to cut, cut, and cut some more. I once read a strategy that I use every time I write: imagine you are paying yourself a dollar for every word you remove. You might share this idea with your students and show them how to remove words to strengthen their work. For example, the first draft might read,

> I remember when we went to the beach last summer. It was sunny. I saw lots and lots of people. Some people were swimming and they were surfing. They were playing in the sand. Some of them were building sandcastles.

After revision, with a focus on removing words, the second draft might look like this:

> At the beach last summer, I saw crowds of people enjoying the sun. Families were swimming, surfing, and building sandcastles.

Show students how to cut out unneeded or repetitive words, and show them how to combine sentences to be more effective.

The Value of Freewriting to Revision

Once your students see how revising can improve their work, they will begin to look forward to this process rather than resist it. In fact, they may be interested to hear that many professional writers find revision to be the most exciting and most critical part of their work. Murray (2004, 1) shares this:

> Do you ever write badly?
> Good. All writers write badly — at first. Nobel Prize winners, Pulitzer Prize winners, writers of blockbuster movies, writers with distinguished academic reputations, writers who influence and persuade, instruct and inspire, comfort and anger and amuse and inform, all write badly. Writers who write novels, speeches, news stories, screenplays, corporate memos, textbooks, plays, poems, history books, scientific reports, legal briefs, grant applications, TV scripts, songs — all write badly — at first.
> Then they rewrite. Revision is not the end of the writing process but the beginning.

This quotation, appropriate to share with your students, can lead to an interesting discussion: in many ways, it helps students understand that revision is both an expected and necessary part of the writing process — for **all** writers. In your classroom, strive to make revision a normal part of the writing process and a positive experience for students.

The power of freewriting in our classrooms becomes clear once again. Students write freely through the process of freewriting. They do not face the dilemma of "I don't know what to write." They get something down on paper in a relatively short time. They know that if they choose they will have an opportunity to revise their work. Freewriting gives them choice in what to revise. Then, in the classroom community of learners, they practise the art of revision, trying new techniques and sharpening the skills that will make their writing shine.

Editing for Conventions

If freewriting becomes a school-wide approach, students will become more familiar with this process from year to year and further develop their editing skills.

The most important thing to remember is that conventions is an area to focus on when we take a particular piece of writing to a final draft. I do not want to compromise my students' ideas during their initial writing. My first goal is to get them writing. Freewriting accomplishes this well. So, often, once freewriting is established, students begin to approach all forms of writing with the same frame of mind. They have less and less difficulty generating ideas because they do not feel bound to or afraid of perfect conventions. It then becomes easier and timelier to teach proper conventions and the process of editing to our students. Through extensive writing with my students, I have discovered that they learn the importance of conventions quite naturally, more naturally than we might expect. Of course, I am directing the conversations and we spend considerable time talking about proper punctuation and spelling to ensure the readability of our work.

I find it helpful to teach my students editing marks for efficiency. After I have introduced them, I post the marks in the classroom for easy reference. Again, they simply serve as a tool that students become accustomed to using. The earlier they are introduced, the better.

We can liberate our students by posting a word wall in the classroom and by not expecting perfect control of the conventions until a final draft. A student who needs more support with phonics and spelling can be given a personal word wall on a folder he puts up on his desk when he is writing. This is not "cheating"; this is supporting a student and enabling him to find success.

In the younger grades, I have a written morning message ready when my students come into class each day. In this message, I tell them about the upcoming day *and* provide a venue for editing practice. Much to my students' delight, I intentionally make errors (spelling, punctuation, repeated words, verb tense, sentence structure): errors that I have recently noticed in my students' writing. At the bottom of the message, I write a number to indicate how many errors I have made. As I point to each word of the message, the students read through it with me. Then, I ask them to raise their hands if they have noticed any mistakes. The mistakes are quite obvious to the students, especially after we have tried reading through the message together. This daily routine is non-threatening editing practice as well as a perfect opportunity to illustrate how difficult it can be to read something without punctuation, for instance. Through this modelling and practice, the students begin to understand that punctuation marks are the traffic signals in our text and that correct spelling is important to convey meaning.

We gather together on the carpet and read the message together. Doing this as a class means that the activity does not become a chore that students dread; instead, it is a time to gather to talk about the day, and it becomes an enjoyable way to teach the students about the importance of proper conventions and editing.

Editing Marks	
Capital letter	≡
End punctuation	⊙ ! ?
Add something	∧
Change to lowercase	/
Take something out	ℓ
Check spelling	sp
Indent	¶

Effective Mentor Texts	Editing for Conventions
Grades 1 to 6	*Exclamation Mark* by Amy Krouse Rosenthal *Eats, Shoots & Leaves: Why, Commas Really Do Make a Difference!* by Lynne Truss *The Girl's Like Spaghetti: Why, You Can't Manage without Apostrophes!* by Lynne Truss *Punctuation Takes a Vacation* by Robin Pulver *Twenty-odd Ducks: Why, Every Punctuation Mark Counts!* by Lynne Truss *Yo! Yes?* by Chris Raschka

As previously discussed, my students do not edit everything they write; I ask them to choose one of every four or five pieces of writing to take to a final stage. One benefit of this practice is that the students do not edit their work the same day it is written. Like most of us, they tend to edit their own work much more effectively when they have time and distance from their writing. In fact, they often laugh at the errors they made at the initial time of writing, mistakes they didn't notice the day they wrote the piece. The distancing also makes the situation much less threatening because they understand that at the time of writing, they were focused on content, not conventions.

Reading Aloud to the Wall

Ultimately, the most effective editing strategy for our student writers is for them to read their work aloud. Teachers have sometimes been surprised to find my students standing around the perimeter of the classroom apparently reading to the walls, paper and pencil in hand. The first few times my students do this, they giggle self-consciously. Quickly though, they realize that it works. There they are reading aloud to the wall, catching mistakes and revising on the spot. After all, "your ear will catch much that your tired eye has missed" (Trimble 1975, 12). I find that reading my writing out loud works best for me, too.

Where Commas Go

The children's version of the book *Eats, Shoots & Leaves* by Lynne Truss is a wonderful way to illustrate the importance of punctuation for students and specifically how a comma, in one place or another, really does change the meaning of the text. For example, the book illustrates (literally) the difference between "Go, get him doctors!" and "Go get him, doctors!" I have seen students spend much time with this book, truly engaged in identifying the differences in comma use and surprised at how the meaning changes. Instead of feeling frustrated while trying to determine where punctuation should go, the students begin to understand (and appreciate) its function and power in their own work.

Intertwining Skill and Subject-Area Teaching

The teaching of writing skills often finds its way into other subject areas. Perhaps your students have been asked to write a persuasive piece in social studies. Your mini-lesson on word choice might fit into your social studies lesson. Not only would you be discussing appropriate language to persuade or convince the reader, but you may also be emphasizing subject-area vocabulary. Or, perhaps your students have created carnival games as part of the probability unit in math. They could create advertisements for the other students in the school, inviting them to come and play the games. Rather than simply having them create quick (and perhaps sloppy) posters, you could teach a mini-lesson on advertisements and presentation. This lesson fits into various areas of the curriculum.

The more intertwined your lessons can be, the better.

11

Emergent Writers: Kindergarten, Grade 1, and Beyond

"The expert in anything was once a beginner."
— Helen Hayes

If you are lucky enough (and some would say, *brave* enough) to teach Kindergarten or Grade 1, you know that the realities of writing in these classrooms are unique. In Kindergarten and Grade 1, more so than at any other grade level, our students are *learning to write*. *Writing to learn* for these youngsters will occur later.

One key goal in Kindergarten and Grade 1 classrooms is the exposure to literacy. Students in these classrooms come to us with varied home experiences and abilities. Some students can identify letters, some understand that letters make sounds, and some understand that the words on a page hold meaning. Others may have very little exposure to the written word. Some of our students may not have access to books in the home or an adult reading a nightly bedtime story. Regardless of their experiences when they get to us, most of these young students haven't yet figured out the mystery of this thing called literacy. For the children who sit before us in our Kindergarten and Grade 1 classrooms, there is often an excitement surrounding words and books.

Awesome Alphabet Books
- *Alphabet City* by Stephen T. Johnson
- *Alphablock* by Christopher Franceschelli
- *Alphaprints: ABC* by Roger Priddy
- *Amazing ABC: An Alphabet Book of Lego Creations* by Sean Kenney
- *Animal Alphabet: Slide & Seek the ABCs* by Alex A. Lluch
- *Chicka Chicka Boom Boom* by Bill Martin Jr. and John Archambault

Astonishing Progress

By surrounding our students with environmental print and quality literature, we can enable them to learn the power of the written word. In Kindergarten, writing often comes in the form of drawing (as discussed in Chapter 5), and guided writing tends to focus on the practice of printing names and the letters of the alphabet. Despite this, the suggestions provided in this chapter are relevant in terms of the environment we create and for those students who show capabilities beyond those of their peers.

Although our Kindergarten students do not engage in writing in the same way as students in other grades, they are involved in all of the other strands of the language arts program, which are incredibly interconnected. As we teach these students to read their names, the environmental print around them, and words in the books we share, they are learning to attend to print cues and begin to recognize words on a page. This is an important step in the development of their writing. As they copy scribed words, they are learning about directionality and spacing between words — both important skills of reading and writing. As they experiment with letter sounds, rhyme, and word families, they are learning the

Common Language Arts Strands
- Listening
- Speaking
- Reading
- Writing
- Viewing
- Representing

basics for emergent writing. As they draw pictures in response to a read-aloud and orally explain their pictures, they are making connections and engaging in an early stage of writing. Eventually, they may begin to emulate the words on a page by creating scribbles or shapes that resemble letters. As they begin to form recognizable letters and print their own names, they exist on the verge of an exciting stage.

I began my career teaching Grade 1. Teaching Grade 1 is unlike any other grade level. The amount of progress a Grade 1 teacher witnesses is exhilarating: from the first beginning attempts at language with a string of letters, to simple sentences with invented spelling and a sprinkling of high-frequency words, and eventually, to a story or journal entry with multiple sentences with profound observations and magnificent, imaginative worlds. The progress is astonishing! And yet, this progress happens every year in Grade 1 classrooms around the world. These students are developmentally ready to tackle this skill called writing.

Stages of Emergent Writing

Both Kindergarten and Grade 1 teachers would benefit from familiarity with the stages of emergent writing to best ensure that they can move their students effectively from one stage to the other. It is important to recognize the elements of the various stages of writing.

Random Marks or Scribbling

At this stage, children recognize that they can make marks on a page. They explore what they can do with a crayon on the paper in the form of random marks or scribbling. Typically, this is what we see of toddlers.

Representational Drawing

Drawing is a child's first form of writing. Even before children are able to write, they are excited about sharing their drawings and telling us about their pictures. Drawings progress through numerous stages with increasing amounts of detail and accuracy. For our purposes, though, a representational drawing goes beyond that of scribbles: we can recognize something in what children have drawn. This child has drawn his family.

Drawing with Distinct Attempts at Writing

As children move through developmental stages, their drawings may begin to include scribbles that resemble writing. For our beginning writers, this is an important step. Though these scribbles don't mean much to us, they are purposeful to the young writer, and they indicate intention. They show that the child recognizes a difference between pictures and words. Eventually, the scribbles will turn into letter-like forms and later into actual letters. This child wrote about her mom, dad, and brother Marcus on the top portion of the page (the lines representing words) and drew a picture of them at the bottom of the page (the circles representing their heads).

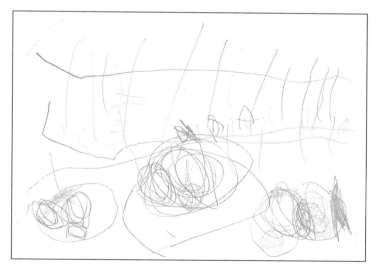

Mock Letters

As they are developmentally ready and after exposure to books and environmental print, children will make scribbles that begin to form shapes resembling letters. Children at this stage are eager to tell you what they have written. This child said he wrote a story about love and sharing.

Letters and Letter Strings

After ongoing exposure to books and the direct teaching of letters and their sounds, children will begin to form actual letters. The letters will not yet be representative of what they want to say, but their presence is something to celebrate! Children at this stage will very often be able to tell you what they wrote. This child said, "I played in the forest at camping."

Invented Spelling

We can liken invented spelling to a child's first attempts at speech. Children do not begin speaking with correct sounds, words, and sentences. The acquisition of speech is a developmental process, much like writing.

Invented spelling is a critical step in a child's writing development. Parents sometimes worry or question invented spelling. However, this stage shows recognition of the relationship between a letter and its sound. Students string letters together with more intention, trying to create particular words and spacing between words. This child completed a reader response after listening to the story *Up the*

Creek by Nicholas Oldland. He wrote, "If I were in a boat I would be the bear and I cannot carry the boat."

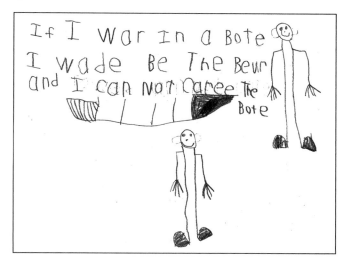

Conventional Spelling

At this stage, high-frequency words and sight words tend to be spelled correctly. Students try to spell more difficult words phonetically. In Grade 1 we begin to teach and encourage conventional spelling through the exploration of words and the use of labels and word walls, for instance. This child wrote, "She searched the whole kingdom. Until she found the beautifulest rose in the land. She went to pick [it]. Until she faced the dreadful beast!"

Students in Different Stages

Kindergarten and Grade 1 teachers recognize that not all children go through these stages at the same rate. Some students are not developmentally ready to recognize the difference between pictures and words, or to form letters. We can certainly involve them in our teaching of the concept and provide experiences and exposure to assist them, but we must realize that these skills may be out of their grasp for some time. And although we encounter most of our emergent writers in Kindergarten and Grade 1, I have taught emergent writers in higher grades as well. We must ensure that we are supporting our students as they move through their developmental stages regardless of their age level and grade.

That being said, where do we begin and how do we move our students through the stages of emergent writing?

Becoming Aware of Print

Young writers need to see the various ways that words are used as a model for their own experimentation with words. *Environmental print* is the print that we encounter in everyday life: street signs, store signs, labels, and logos. Teaching students to become observant of the environmental print around them helps to confirm the idea that words hold meaning.

Labels All around the Room

When I taught Grade 1, I labelled my desk, the clock, the bookshelf, the ceiling, the windows, the door, and the floor. I was amazed at the number of times students referred to these labels. Simply by surrounding them with words, we motivate and excite students to attempt their own written language. Students are easily able to read the labels in our classrooms because they are directly connected to the objects. Though most of our Kindergarten and Grade 1 students cannot yet sound out the word *window*, they understand what word it is simply because of the location of the label. I often observe my students jumping out of their desks during writing time to find the label for door or desk. They confidently include these words in their writing: they are empowered by the labels.

If you adopt the practice of labelling items in your classroom, you can also have students who are further along in their literacy development help you with this process. Just be sure that their printing is readable and correct.

Letter or Word Search

I call my students "letter detectives" (Kindergarten and early Grade 1) or "word detectives" (later Grade 1) as we walk through the school on the hunt for a particular letter or sight word. Students can bring pointers, use pretend magnifying glasses, or simply wield their pointer fingers as they find the particular letter or word we are studying. This simple activity draws attention to the environmental print around the school, something that some students walk by every day without noticing. It also helps students to realize that letters and words are all around us and that letters are the building blocks for words.

Songs and Mentor Texts

We teach our students from a very young age to read as writers. If we use familiar songs, students can begin to track the printed words. As they track the words they are saying, they may not be able to read all of the words, but they are making important connections. They learn that each word said matches a word on the page. They begin to recognize high-frequency words. Familiar songs or rhymes like "Five Little Monkeys" or repetitive books like *Brown Bear, Brown Bear, What Do You See?* assist students in making these associations.

Taking a sentence frame from one of these songs or books could be the basis for a shared writing experience. Brainstorming together as a class, students could write their own version of the song or story. Then, each student would be responsible for printing the words of one line of the story or song (and illustrating it) on a single page. All of the single pages would then be combined to create a special class book.

If we build their self-confidence as readers, our students will become more willing writers.

Discovering Basic Conventions of Print

Once our students recognize print we can teach them the basic conventions of print: directionality and spacing, upper case and lower case letters, and punctuation.

Directionality and Spacing

Although the concepts seem simple, it is necessary to teach students to write from left to right and to use proper spacing between words. Students who have been exposed to many books tend to adopt these practices quite easily. Students who were not read to on a regular basis or who did not have access to many books as a preschooler may find these concepts more difficult to grasp.

We model directionality when we read morning messages or shared texts with our students. Students can take turns using a pointer to track the words while the class reads aloud.

We must also model proper spacing. When writing in front of our students, we use the technique of finger spacing so our students can do the same. Spacing between words indicates that a student understands the concept of a word.

In Kindergarten we provide blank paper to our students and avoid pages with lines, while in Grade 1, we begin to provide interlined paper. By this point students typically have the fine motor control required to control the size and spacing of their printing. The dotted line between the solid lines is an important indicator for our emergent writers. However, you will likely have a few students in your class who are not yet ready for proper spacing: their fine motor control is not yet developed and their printing is likely quite large. These students would benefit from paper without any lines. At this stage we celebrate the success of proper letter formations as they occur. We move to interlined paper for these youngsters when they seem ready.

Upper Case and Lower Case

In Kindergarten, we teach the students the letters of the alphabet, both upper case and lower case. When they are learning to write their names, we stress the use of an upper case letter to begin their names and lower case letters for the remainder of their names. We draw attention to upper case letters at the beginning of sentences and proper names when reading aloud. Students in Kindergarten are not

Too often, I notice students in older grades using improper cases: upper case letters in the middle of words, lower case letters at the beginning of the sentence, a lower case *i* for the word *I*. More often than not, these are simply bad habits the students have developed. These habits can be broken, but they require the efforts of a persistent teacher!

typically transferring this to their own writing but the discussion is important to set the stage for Grade 1.

By Grade 1, most students will have learned to recognize most letters of the alphabet. Our Grade 1 classrooms should have an alphabet displayed on the wall and also on each student desk for easy reference. Most name tags we put on student desks in Grade 1 have an alphabet and numbers for student reference. Teaching students to use the proper upper and lower case letters is important: focus especially on letters at the beginning of sentences and of proper nouns.

Punctuation

Sometimes while reading out loud to my students, I playfully read as if there is no punctuation. Students begin to appreciate its necessity when it becomes hard to understand what I am reading — the sentences all run together!

While reading mentor texts, teach punctuation as something effective writers use to help us understand what they are trying to say. This way, it becomes a given. *Writers use punctuation; you are a writer and, therefore, you use punctuation, too.*

It is helpful to equate punctuation marks to traffic signs. A period is represented by a stop sign and tells the reader to come to a full stop. A comma is represented by a yield sign and tells the reader to slow down and pause slightly. Students in Grade 1 will also begin to use exclamation marks and question marks effectively.

Sometimes, I ask students to count the number of sentences on a page in a mentor text. To ensure that all students are trying to figure out the answer, they wait with their hands up before sharing. This simple task shows that students can identify the beginning and end of a sentence. After I have asked a few students to share their answers, we count the sentences together as a class. If I ever ask students to write three sentences in their journals, for instance, they now know how to create them and count them.

One of my favorite books to spark a conversation about punctuation with my Grade 1 students is *Yo! Yes?* by Chris Raschka. This book has few words per page but it employs very intentional punctuation that helps students understand the difference between a statement, an exclamation, and a question. Students enjoy reading this simple text over and over, practising proper inflection. After reading this book, my students and I write a class book using the same concept of a few simple, repeated words.

As Grade 1 teachers can attest, punctuation is a daily discussion point!

Exploring and Experimenting with Words

As students become more familiar with print and its conventions, they begin attempting their own written language. Even without being asked, emergent writers will add letters to their pictures. There are many things we can do as teachers to encourage this practice.

The Teaching of Phonics

Typically in Kindergarten our work with phonics is demonstration and direct teaching. Students recite chants and songs about the letters and their sounds.

Parts and Wholes
Phonics is the method of learning to read by sounding out words, breaking each whole into parts. Whole language instruction, in contrast, focuses on deriving meaning from the written word in an environment where children are surrounded by literature and print.

Words that are *not* high-frequency are treated much differently than our high-frequency words. For example, if a student attempted to write the word *elephant* and did not come up with standard spelling, I would not correct it. The student would not yet be expected to spell this word correctly.

Word Family Lists
Phonemic awareness is the ability to hear, identify, and manipulate the individual sounds in words. Word families are an effective strategy for building on phonemic awareness and vastly increasing our students' written vocabulary. In fact, posting lists of word families (ideally generated by the students — not store-bought) can be a useful reference for students in addition to a word wall.

They search for the letters, identify the letters, and begin to learn the sounds that letters make. Most often it is in Grade 1 that students will be able to transfer this knowledge and understanding into their own writing.

Writing in Grade 1 holds a power all its own. We continue to build on the momentum begun by Kindergarten teachers with a focus on phonics. Though the pendulum tends to swing back and forth between phonics and whole language, I have always found it helpful to teach using a combination of the two approaches. I believe that most students need a background in phonics in order to become effective writers.

In Grade 1, we strive to have our students move from a string of random letters to letters that reflect the sounds in the words they want to communicate. We certainly cannot expect them to have perfect spelling as they are learning to write: that expectation is sure to stifle them. By providing our students with short sentence starters, we can scaffold their beginning writing. For example, students can use sentence beginnings such as "I can …" or "I want …" Such prompts can guide students' early writing. Students can also refer to the labels and other environmental print around the classroom. As they begin to take risks to try to spell unknown words, students will use invented spelling and basic phonics to write the words on the page. Praise these attempts.

Our goal is to encourage student efforts to spell as a means to convey what they want to say. Tony Stead (2002) affirms, "As teachers we need to find effective methods to encourage children to approximate — to try spelling words they want to use — so that their message becomes paramount in their writing, and is not governed solely by spelling" (72). One way of doing this is to encourage students to utilize the classroom word wall and do their best to spell words independently. Whenever possible, we can scaffold attempts at spelling more difficult words, for example, when writing something on the board or on chart paper with the whole class. The think-aloud process will assist students when they are working individually. By helping them focus on message over standard spelling, we will hear less of what's likely the most common question in a Grade 1 classroom: "How do you spell _____?"

Word Work

Word work activities can help our beginning writers feel more confident attempting words in their writing. I provide regular word work activities but I vary the method to ensure I reach all students and maintain student engagement. On some days, I use letter cards that students can manipulate into words that I guide them to create. On other days, we use magnetic letters. Sometimes, we use mini whiteboards and markers. Regardless of the materials, these activities are empowering for young writers.

I may begin by asking students to spell the word *hat*. I sound it out with them, carefully emphasizing each of the sounds: h-a-t. Then, I tell them that if they can spell *hat*, they can also spell *cat*. "Take away the *h* and put a *c*." I ensure that they all have the letters in the correct order. "You just spelled *cat*! C-a-t. Cat!" I then tell them that if they can spell *cat*, they can also spell *bat*. And so on. They begin to move from the known to the unknown, building confidence each step of the way.

Sometimes during word work, I have students sort words according to beginning sounds or word families. This is best accomplished if students can manipulate the words themselves. Word cards are ideal for this purpose.

A favorite word work activity for students is something I call Word Work Challenge. Students are given a list of 10 letters. Their goal is to create as many words as they can, using some or all of those letters. I am always amazed to see how something so simple can generate such excitement!

These same word work activities can also be organized as centres whereby we can differentiate for the various ability levels within the classroom. I find it effective to work with small groups of students as they rotate through the centres. I can provide direct instruction at the level of my students.

The beauty of word work activities is that students view them as fun and you can continuously build on your students' understanding of phonics. In addition to initial sounds and word families, you can work on consonant blends (e.g., *bl*, *br*, *cl*, *cr*, *dr*, *fr*, *gl*, *gr*, *pr*, *sl*, *sm*, *sp*, *st*, *tr*), diagraphs (e.g., *ch*, *sh*, *th*, *wh*), vowel sounds, suffixes, homonyms, and so on.

A Wall of Words

In your classroom set aside a prominent, easily accessible space for a word wall. Prepare the word wall before the students arrive on the first day but do not put up any words. If words are already on the word wall, the students will likely feel overwhelmed and not refer to the words because they cannot yet read them. Rather, build the word wall with the students. Each week, add new words and discuss them. Ideally, reference the words in a shared text and have students work with the words before you put them up.

In Kindergarten, our word walls are limited to the names of the students in our class and some high-frequency words. Some teachers use pictures to accompany the words on a Kindergarten word wall. For example, a child's name would also include a picture of the child. This scaffolding will help ensure that all our students can access these words.

In Grade 1, in addition to student names, begin adding high-frequency words to the word wall (no more than two or three words at a time) as early as the first week of school. These become the words students are expected to spell correctly. As this list grows, students are continually adding to their repertoire for both reading and writing.

If a student writes a sentence and I notice that the word *big* is spelled incorrectly and it is already on our word wall, I will underline the word and put a small *ww* in pencil. This indicates to the student that the word is on the word wall and he or she is to go back and fix it. I playfully refer to the word wall in my Grade 1 classroom as the *No-Excuse-Word-Wall* because if a word is on the wall, there is no excuse for misspelling it. Very quickly students get into the habit of referring to the word wall for assistance. This promotes independence in their writing and curbs the habit of students coming to the teacher every time they try to spell a word.

Refer to the word wall in your classroom often so your students develop the habit of using it during their writing time. Play activities or games with the word-wall words. For example, as part of your weekly routine, your Student of the Day could choose a word from the word wall and the other students could ask questions to try to figure out what the word is. "Does the word have more than three letters?" "Does the word begin with a vowel?" As you can imagine, this activity is good practice both for those asking the questions and for the student who chose the word. Support the Student of the Day to ensure that the questions are answered correctly.

Ever wondered about the difference between blends and diagraphs? In a blend, you still hear the original sounds of each letter, as in /sl/. In a diagraph, the letters come together to create a new sound, for example, /ch/.

The class word wall might overwhelm your low literacy students, so consider creating small personal word walls that these students can refer to. A personal word wall could be as simple as five high-frequency words listed on a student's desk.

Many teachers use the idea of a Student of the Day or Star Student. The Student of the Day is given special duties such as serving as line leader or classroom messenger.

Seasonal Word Walls

In addition to the regular word wall that we use throughout the year, I have also found it effective to create a bulletin board with words connected to a theme or our curricular content. If it is Halloween or if we are studying the five senses, I post words connected to these topics on the seasonal word wall. Often student writing will be connected to these topics, and this seasonal word wall can be an effective resource for the students.

When I tell the students about an upcoming curricular topic, I ask them to brainstorm a list of words that they associate with the topic. As they say them, I write them on the board or on chart paper. When we are finished, I pull out my prepared words for this word wall. I build the anticipation for each word and then together we check to see if my word is a word they have brainstormed. Rather than my saying the word, we figure it out together and try to match it to the list of words they have created. This becomes an anticipated activity for students each time we change the seasonal word wall.

What It's All About: New Words!

When students begin to notice interesting word choice in literature, they tend to use more interesting words in their own writing. When teachers include a high-frequency word wall and a seasonal word wall in the classroom, and set a supportive tone, students will feel more confident attempting words that they may not know how to spell. It's all in our approach.

We want our students to improve their writing. Therefore, it is appropriate to write the correct spelling above their attempts *occasionally* but not for every word on the page. Of course, if our students are continually told that their spelling is wrong, they will be less inclined to try to spell a more difficult word the next time. If we acknowledge their attempts at correct spelling and encourage more of the same, students will be more likely to try new words. And let's face it, in Kindergarten and Grade 1, that's what it's all about: new words!

A Book of Favorite Words

In my experience, young students love little things. I buy each of my Grade 1 students a little coil memo book (3 by 5 inches). This book becomes their book of favorite words. I simply encourage them to add to their notebooks when they find a word they like. I comment on interesting words when I encounter them and this is often enough to motivate students to do the same.

Students could share their notebooks with their reading buddies or with parents during a demonstration of learning. By sharing, they are practising their reading skills and perhaps explaining their choice of words.

Transition Words

In Grade 1, emergent writing can sometimes be quite repetitive, using the same sentence beginnings over and over — *and* and *then* are common first words. Students benefit from a lesson in transition words. These words help structure student writing and provide a sequence. What *are* transition words? *First, next, then, finally.* If you provide simple graphic organizers with these transition words,

If a student asks me how to spell *haunted house* and I know it is on the word wall, I will direct her to look for it there. Usually, a conversation ensues about beginning sounds. "Haunted house — hmmm … what sound do you hear at the beginning? Right. And what letter makes that sound? An *h*! That's right. Actually, I hear two *h*'s — haunted house." Not only is this conversation helping a student with reading skills, but also with writing.

Eventually in Grade 1 we have conversations about nouns, verbs, and adjectives. By our introducing these concepts early, students begin to understand their definitions and purpose. Over the course of the school year, I create anchor charts with the students that we then post for student reference.

students will become more familiar with their use. Students can either draw pictures in each of the boxes or write simple sentences depending on their level.

First	Next	Then	Finally

Writing with Purpose and Pride

Over and over I have been privileged to experience the wonder in children as they first realize that words on a page hold meaning. At this precious age, students want to write. We must capitalize on their enthusiasm and scaffold their learning along the way.

Question of the Day

Some Kindergarten students may be ready for Question of the Day by the end of the year.

There are several ways to make writing in Grade 1 purposeful. One option is to provide a Question of the Day. As students come into the classroom each morning, they pick up a strip of paper, write their name (good practice in and of itself), and write the answer to the Question of the Day that you put on the board. This activity will provide good reading practice and also writing practice. Students tend to look forward to the question each day!

Students will be able to do more over time. At the beginning of the year, you might expect a one-word answer. You could even have the sentence starter on the strip of paper so students see the full sentence. As the year goes on, students would be expected to write complete sentences. Question examples:

- Who is your friend?
- How are you feeling today?
- What game do you like to play?
- What is your favorite place?
- Who do you live with?
- What is the best part about you?
- What do you think is in outer space?
- What are you scared of?
- What is the worst smell in the world?
- What are you thankful for?
- What superpower do you wish you had?
- What is your favorite word?
- What is the greatest thing ever invented?
- What do you like to do on Saturdays?
- What makes you cry?
- What is the best part about Grade 1?
- If all your clothes had to be one color, what color would they be?
- If you had to eat one thing for the rest of your life, what would it be?
- What do you want to be when you grow up?
- What's the hardest thing about being a kid?

Sample return slip:

Name: _____

I ate _____ for breakfast today.

Modelled Writing

As noted in Chapter 10, I write a morning message to my primary students each day. In doing so, I tell them about the upcoming day, model effective writing, and also provide a venue for editing practice. I intentionally make errors: errors that I have recently noticed in my students' writing. This is non-threatening editing practice and a perfect opportunity to illustrate how difficult it can be to read something without punctuation. Through this modelling and practice, the students are helped to understand that punctuation marks are the traffic signals in our text and that correct spelling is important to convey meaning. We gather together on the carpet and read the message together.

Talk as Prewriting

Don't worry that the ideas will be the same. We simply want them writing!

For many young students, talk is a precursor to writing — after all, oral language precedes written language. Before asking our emergent writers to write, it is important to provide them with time to talk and listen to others. I often gather my students on the carpet for a whole-class discussion before our writing time. An alternative is to have them talk to their tablemates to share ideas. Whatever approach we take, their writing will likely include more details as a result of the talk, and they probably will not say, "I don't have anything to write about." Typically, by talking about the topic first, students feel more confident trying to put words on paper: they now know what they want to say.

The Use of Pictures

In Grade 1, you may have students who are not yet ready to attempt writing. For them, journal and reader response entries are still primarily pictures. As is done for Kindergarten journal entries (see Chapter 5), students can dictate a word or a sentence that you then write under a picture. Eventually, they will attempt the language on their own but be sure to move at their pace, scaffolding along the way.

As our students become writers, teachers sometimes expect them to write first and draw the picture second. And yet, some young students are more successful when they draw their picture *before* writing in their journal or *before* writing a story. They formulate their ideas through their drawings: the details in the picture then become the basis of the writing. As outlined in Chapter 6, students are encouraged to draw a storyboard or complete a graphic organizer as planning for their stories. Ultimately, as long as they are writing, it should not matter if they drew their pictures first.

Writing through the Year

As shared earlier, whenever I teach Grade 1, I find myself excited to watch the progress the students make with their writing. We begin the year writing in journals with various prompts and by responding to literature. By November, I teach my students about transformation stories and we begin our first narrative stories. December tends to be a good time of year to write our first letter (to Santa Claus, of course) and letter writing can continue later in the year, perhaps to a favorite author. By January, I introduce freewriting to my Grade 1 students. Throughout the year we write journal entries, reader responses, and narrative stories.

Giving and Receiving Feedback

If we teach our students to share their work, provide feedback to others, and accept feedback from their peers, they will see writing as practical and interactive from a very young age. I begin the use of writing groups with students as young as Grade 1.

For the first few months of Grade 1, I model the expectations of sharing and giving feedback in a whole-class setting. These youngsters are characteristically very honest, which can be a positive feature when giving feedback. We simply must teach them how to provide feedback tactfully. Typically, by January, the students are ready to move into writing groups, as explained in Chapter 1.

Publishing Student Work

Posting student work around the classroom shows that we value their writing. Invite students to share their writing often and encourage students to read each other's work during independent reading time.

Another form of publishing student work involves using an authentic audience. Perhaps the students are writing to thank the secretary or custodian. Or, perhaps they are writing to ask something of the principal. As a teacher, you can use these authentic audiences to encourage students to do their best work.

Assessment: All about Feedback

Regardless of the form of writing, assessment in Kindergarten and Grade 1 is all about feedback! The tone you use with your students, both written and verbal, is most important. Expectations should be high — upper case letters at the beginning of our names, for example — but it is essential that we maintain a positive attitude for these beginning writers. If we want our students to take risks, we must praise their efforts and respect their current level of ability.

Student Portfolios

In Kindergarten especially, student work is often completed on single pages and then sent home. The absence of a scribbler, duotang, or binder makes it more difficult to compare work from one month to another, as we do in higher grades. A good idea is to create individual portfolios for your students, saving one or two samples a month!

In both Kindergarten and Grade 1, it is powerful to keep biweekly or monthly writing samples in individual student portfolios. This work, dated to show progress, becomes a remarkable record of our students' development: interesting for parents, teachers, and even the students.

As the year progresses in Grade 1, I begin to use rubrics to help guide student writing even further. We talk continually about what makes good writing and work towards improving various aspects of our writing. Students at this age are easily motivated to improve their work!

12

Reaching Our English Language Learners and Reluctant Writers

"If a child can't learn the way we teach, maybe we should teach the way they learn."
— Ignacio Estrada

Whether you have English language learners (ELLs) in your class or students who either dislike or fear writing, you may need to differentiate your lessons to meet their needs. The beauty of teaching writing is that students work at their own ability levels. The writing is both an end goal (*learning to write*) and a process of learning (*writing to learn*).

Consider how much our ELLs are learning every moment of the day. They are surrounded by both conversational English and academic English. They are exposed to an extensive amount of new vocabulary. They are learning the nuances of language: the rules, the exceptions, the structure, the grammar, the syntax, not to mention pronunciation. They are learning to listen, speak, read, and write. What an overwhelming and exhausting task! Therefore, in order to support our ELLs, we must ensure that they have direct language instruction regardless of the grades they are in. These are not cognitively challenged students — they are simply challenged because of circumstance.

Recognizing Student Fears

When I imagine myself in a classroom full of individuals speaking an unfamiliar language, I feel like fading into the background. For me, a foreign classroom would be a stressful environment. The thought of being asked to say something in an unfamiliar language terrifies me. The expectation to *write* something frightens me even more! We must remember that this is how many of our ELLs feel in our classrooms. For many of them, not only is the language new, but so are the culture, the climate, and the school system with its rules, routines, and expectations.

Once again, then, we must acknowledge the importance of developing a strong community of learners: a classroom in which ELLs feel safe enough to take risks and attempt language. As teachers, we can work to create as welcoming and low stress an environment as possible for students new to our country and our classrooms. We want them to feel comfortable asking questions and supported as they try to share their own thoughts and ideas.

In addition to ELLs, many teachers ask how to support their reluctant writers. At different ages for different individuals, some students begin to fear or even dread writing. In dialogue with students over the years, I have found that ELLs and reluctant writers tend to have similar fears: fear of failure, fear of someone reading their work, fear of making mistakes, fear of incorrect spelling, punctuation, or grammar. Writing, after all, makes us vulnerable. If, when our students are writing, they thought no one would read their work, they would likely feel more comfortable and worry less about the end product. Often, in the younger grades, the students are excited for us to read their work and tell us about their pictures. As our students become older, many of them become more self-conscious about their writing, particularly if they doubt they are very good at it.

Strategies to Ensure Fair Treatment

By using the strategies and forms of writing outlined in this book, you should, I hope, be able to limit the number of reluctant writers in your classroom. Especially by establishing the practice of freewriting, I was often able to reduce the need for further intervention. How? Freewriting, in particular, addresses many of the concerns of the writers in our classrooms. It eliminates the worry about correct spelling, punctuation, and grammar. It eliminates the worry about someone reading their work. Freewriting was the game changer for me in my classroom. But the other strategies, too, help all students feel more successful. For example, providing plot patterns or a framework supports all writers; guided writing, mini-lessons, and individual conferencing serve as scaffolding for our students; and writing groups provide the peer support and oral communication necessary for students to improve their writing.

So, although these strategies help meet the needs of all students, be aware of students who need more support and more deliberate instruction than others. Remember that *fair* does not mean treating all students equally; *fair* means supporting our students based on their individual needs. The following strategies can be useful for elementary students of any age.

Hold Morning Meetings

As I described in Chapter 1, consider gathering each day for a morning meeting. These meetings are effective for all students, but they can be especially beneficial for our ELLs. The expected routine can be comforting as they are encountering things new to them throughout every day. In addition, by participating in morning meetings, they become more familiar with the structure of language, the format of questions and answers, and the expectations of listening and of talking in turn. In faith-based schools, this time can also be time for prayer and intentions. These class meetings become a safe place for our students to experiment with oral language which will ultimately help them with their writing as well.

Engage in Prewriting Discussion: Talk Time

Most of us are familiar with the value of pre-reading activities for our struggling readers and ELLs; however, prewriting discussion — talk time, put simply — can be valuable to all writers. Not only might students hear new vocabulary or correct misconceptions, but talk time is also helpful in generating ideas for their writing. By talking about something first, they begin to sort through their thoughts, making it easier to put them down on paper or screen.

Build this talk time into your regular writing schedule. When giving a topic or prompt, have students turn to the person beside them and simply talk about it first. If, on occasion, you want students to just go ahead and write, be sure to retain the talk time for your ELLs and reluctant writers.

Differentiate Assignment Length and Expectations

Although you might think that differentiating assignment length and expectations is a given, I have witnessed teachers who expect all students in their class, regardless of their background or ability, to complete assignments to the same standards. This is simply unrealistic, sure to dampen the spirit and efforts of those who find learning more difficult or those new to the language.

Recently I came across a comment written by a teacher in a student's journal which made me want to cry: *"Your sentences are a bunch of random thoughts with no flow."* I don't know the teacher. The journal came in the student's file and we were asked to pass it along to him. This student had arrived in Canada only a few months prior. I read the student's writing and was impressed with both the quantity and the quality of his work for a student new to the English language. The teacher seemed to be judging based on her expectations of her typical Grade 5 students. If *I* felt deflated when I read that comment, imagine how the student felt.

Be flexible and fluid in your expectations. Be wary of saying to a student "write five sentences" and then never varying that expectation or challenging him to write more. Rather than making the length of an assignment the criterion, focus on the content.

While students are writing, get into the habit of checking in with your ELLs and reluctant writers. Read what they have written partway through the assignment and then engage in a brief conversation or ask questions about the topic to generate more ideas. Doing this is often enough to motivate them to keep writing a little more. You need not do this during a freewrite, but it can be useful for all other types of written assignments.

Provide More Scaffolding

Students who struggle with language often benefit from more scaffolding for the tasks they encounter. This could be done through access to sentence starters, sentence frames, a personal word wall (on a writing folder, at the beginning of their scribbler, or on their desk), or graphic organizers.

Whether students are going to complete a journal entry, a reader response, or a freewrite in science, I keep a list of simple prompts visible for them to access anytime. Some writers are more comfortable when they have a framework even on a task that we consider more open-ended. Here are a few effective prompts for this purpose:

- I first thought …
- I learned …
- I wonder about …
- I have a question about …
- I liked when …
- This reminded me of …

Scaffolding can also come in the form of repeated instructions or step-by-step written instructions for our students. The majority of the class (though I wonder about this sometimes) may understand our multi-step instructions the first time we give them. But clear language and simple, step-by-step instructions will likely benefit many students. Giving auditory instructions is typical; providing visual instructions, as well, is recommended. You can write down your instructions on the whiteboard or Smartboard. Doing so provides students with the opportunity to check back as they move through various steps.

Our ELLs often smile and nod so we might assume they understand. We shouldn't. After giving whole-class instructions, check in with your ELLs individually and give the instructions again simply and directly. A peer could also be asked to provide this form of scaffolding.

Model and Model Again

When I am doing something for the first time — no matter what it is — I like to see someone do the task first so I can see how it is done most effectively. The same is true for writing in our classrooms. As discussed throughout this book, modelling is an essential experience for all students. Our ELLs and reluctant writers might require further modelling either in a small group or individually. What are we modelling? Anything really: sequencing our ideas, using conjunctions (*and, but, if*) within our writing, using a variety of sentence beginnings, even editing. We certainly cannot expect our students to learn something after one demonstration: plan for *ongoing* modelling.

Build on Background Knowledge

We all have background knowledge: our daily experiences since birth have created this knowledge about our world. The more we can build on background knowledge for our students and the more we can connect to their own lives, the better. This is effective for all students, of course, but perhaps most effective for those who struggle or who are new to the language. How do we do this? Encouraging students to make connections to the content we teach (text to text, text to self, text to world), the discussions we have, and the texts we read will assist them when it comes time to write. The more that students have knowledge about a topic, the more effectively they can understand and then elaborate on their understandings. The less background knowledge they have on a given topic, the more abstract (and, therefore, the more difficult) the learning.

The background knowledge of your ELLs may be significantly different than that of the other children in your class, but your choice of mentor text can take this into account. As mentioned in Chapter 2, whenever possible, choose mentor texts that reflect the various cultures in your classroom (see "Mentor Texts with a Cultural Component" on page 24). Reading aloud texts that students can connect with and see themselves reflected in provides them with an opportunity to talk about their own experiences. Honor these experiences and encourage the students to contribute to your discussions. What a wonderful learning experience for all the students in your class! The ELLs will have the opportunity to practise their oral language skills and feel included in your classroom, and the other students will glimpse a world likely unknown to them. Keep in mind, though, it takes time for ELLs to feel comfortable sharing in front of the class. They are more likely to do so when they feel supported, accepted, and connected.

After I read the book *Goal!* by Mina Javaherbin to a Grade 6 class, one student shared his personal connection to the text. Just as one of the characters in the book had to walk to the well for water every day, he, too, in his home in Sudan, had had to do the same. He also shared that they didn't have a soccer ball; instead, they played with a plastic bottle. His sharing prompted other students to contribute, and many articulated how lucky they were to live in Canada.

You can also build background knowledge by bringing in real objects or showing pictures or videos to support the learning. I once brought a couple of pomegranates into class to cut and eat when I realized that the reading selection would be difficult to understand if students were unfamiliar with this fruit. I learned two lessons from doing this: first, all students benefited from this hands-on experience; and second, showing the pomegranates led to an interesting discussion about various types of fruit throughout the world. My ELLs were sharing excitedly!

Keep Teaching Word Patterns and Families

For young writers, one of the stumbling blocks is spelling. Although freewriting helps students break through that barrier, we can also help students understand words better by teaching about patterns, chunking, blends, word families, and root words. Recognizing patterns and word families can help students become more confident readers and writers. I tell my students, "If you can spell *ball*, you can spell *call*, *fall*, *mall*, *stall*, and *tall*." These concepts are naturally included in our primary classrooms as students are learning to read. In older grades these discussions still need to occur to assist all students, especially our ELLs and reluctant writers, with the development of their spelling. Depending on your grade and the specific needs of your students, this intentional teaching may be done in small groups rather than with the whole class.

Subject-Area Vocabulary: Cause for Accommodation

Our ELLs and reluctant writers may especially need support in subject areas with content-area vocabulary and in subjects with more abstract concepts. Make the necessary accommodations to support these students, for example, oral tests, a reader, a scribe, and the use of pictures. As well, the strategies presented in this chapter can be used across the curriculum to assist our ELLs and reluctant writers. Keep in mind that there is often a wide gap between what the students know and what they can communicate.

Deliberate Teaching of Vocabulary

Students need to understand many levels of vocabulary to function in a classroom setting: conversational vocabulary, academic vocabulary, and content-related vocabulary. We cannot assume that our students know all of the words we are using. Nor can we assume that our students know the meaning of a word in a given context.

The English language is riddled with multiple meanings that can be awfully confusing for those learning English. Consider these examples: *bark* (a dog barks; the bark of a tree), *nails* (fingernails; nails and a hammer), *mine* (it is mine; a diamond mine or a coal mine), *bolt* (a lightning bolt; a metal fastener; to run away quickly), and *tie* (to tie your shoes; a shirt and tie). We won't even go into the many meanings of the word *run* ... How perplexing for individuals new to English!

If our students cannot understand the vocabulary that is spoken or read, they cannot use it properly in their speech or written language. It is important to talk about the words we encounter in our reading. Sometimes I do this before reading a selection, sometimes as we read, and sometimes afterwards. Regardless, we should be cognizant of what vocabulary might be difficult for our students. New vocabulary will likely be attempted in speech before it is used in writing. This is another reason to ensure that our students have time to talk.

Deliberate vocabulary instruction will assist students in understanding the curriculum you are teaching in all subject areas. Avoid giving students a list of words. Plan ahead and look for vocabulary that will likely be difficult or simply unfamiliar to your ELLs. Planned exposure to words as well as explicit teaching of words is vital. I use several strategies to teach vocabulary words: word walls, labels, picture dictionaries, personal dictionaries, and real-world examples.

Subject-Area Word Walls

Just as I create word walls in my Grade 1 classroom, I find it helpful to create a content-driven word wall if ELLs are in the class. I have seen some teachers of upper elementary students effectively divide their word wall into sections: high-frequency words, science, social studies, mathematics, and so on. Some teachers include all words on one word wall, but color-code the various subject areas. Generally, in my classroom, I prefer to have a bulletin board for each subject and a portion of the bulletin board devoted to the content vocabulary we are currently studying. There are many ways to organize a word wall: find the method that works in your classroom.

For our ELLs it is effective to include pictures of the words whenever possible. Doing this works easily for a noun like *flag* but is a little more challenging for a word like *democracy*. Consider involving students in creating the words and pictures for your word wall, setting high expectations for legibility.

A Labelled Classroom

Whenever possible, I use word labels throughout the classroom. Through labels, students are exposed to these words repeatedly, which helps with both retention and understanding. If you are concerned that the other students will find this too juvenile in their classroom, remind them what it would be like to be in a class where they don't speak the language. Giving them this perspective quickly makes the use of labels an acceptable practice. In fact, my non-ELLs often become excited about helping their peers and take on the responsibility of labelling around the room.

Picture Dictionaries

I provide my ELLs with a picture dictionary that they can access throughout the year. For very young students, my favorite is Usborne's *First Hundred Words in English*. For older students, I prefer *The Heinle Picture Dictionary for Children*. My ELLs enjoy flipping through these books in their free time. Picture dictionaries allow students to discover new words at their own pace and in areas of interest. Most picture dictionaries are organized by theme or category. I do not typically use these dictionaries for students to look up how to spell the words. However, as they become familiar with the books, I have found students searching for a word they are trying to spell if they remembered seeing it in the book beforehand. Picture dictionaries can be a powerful learning tool.

Personal Dictionaries

Students can create their own personal dictionaries. Within the dictionaries, they write the word to be defined and then use a combination of words and pictures to demonstrate the word's meaning. After I introduced this to my ELLs one year, I then found it was something all students wanted to do and ultimately benefited from. It became a reference and study guide for our content vocabulary and often echoed the word wall we created.

These dictionaries can be created on index cards, on a tablet, in a visual journal, or in a scribbler. Some students prefer the index cards because they can then create flaps that hide the picture and definition. Encourage students to get into the habit of underlining the root word if there is one. Learning to identify the root word will ultimately help them understand the meaning of the word and its connection to other words.

Real-World Examples

Using real-world examples, such as the pomegranates referred to earlier in the chapter, is also helpful. Students are more likely to remember the meaning of the word *pomegranate* once they have seen, touched, smelled, and, in this case, tasted one!

Assessment: Personalize It

When it comes time for formative assessment, give a little extra attention to your ELLs and reluctant writers. Provide more comments and specific feedback than you would with the other students. Anything that is personalized will help to motivate them and provide them with guidance as they move forward with their work.

We can't expect any student to master something on the first try. This is especially true for our reluctant writers and ELLs. So, schedule conferences a little more frequently and check-in informally more often. When responding with written feedback on student work, be positive as well as specific in your suggestions for improvement. The added benefits? These students will begin to feel accepted and at least partially understood in their new surroundings.

13

Daring to Begin …

"All glory comes from daring to begin."
— Eugene F. Ware

Why did you become a teacher? What was it that inspired you to choose this challenging profession? Unless you are a teacher (or married to one), it is difficult to grasp the many hours that go into the planning and preparation, the assessments and report cards. Unless you are a teacher, it is difficult to understand the challenges of meeting the diverse needs of the students before you each day. Unless you are a teacher, it is difficult to appreciate the physical and emotional toll of the job. But, like most in this profession, you presumably chose to teach because you love children, and you aspire to make a difference in their lives.

So, what better gift can you give them than literacy? I would argue none. Literacy skills are essential regardless of the direction our students take in life. The literacy skills we teach will assist our students throughout their schooling and beyond: whether they are filling out job applications, communicating in their professional lives, or reading stories to their own children in years to come.

> "We are not 'just' teachers, we are the managers of the world's greatest resource: children!"
> — Robert John Meehan

Perhaps you are a beginning teacher, eager to teach your first group of students. Or, perhaps you have a long career behind you but your students continue to delight and surprise you. Regardless, you read this book and wonder — as all good teachers do — *how can I make my teaching a little better?* How?

Begin by providing memorable literacy moments.

Providing Memorable Literacy Moments

My first literacy moments occurred at home under the covers of my bed when I was a small child. Nothing could shake our bedtime routine: I would choose three books from the shelf, and my parents would take turns reading to me as I munched on my nightly apple. Not only the books drew me into literacy but also the experiences and relationships surrounding it. Mem Fox explains:

> I'm certain that learning to read and learning to love reading owe a great deal (much more than we ever dreamed) to the *nature of the human relationships* that occur around and through books. If we could sneak into the homes of avid readers, I think we'd discover very often that the comfortable relationship between an older reader and a younger reader during the shared reading of a mutually loved book might be a key factor in the child's success. (1993, 136)

Some of our students have these same cherished moments with their own families, but others may not. As teachers, though, we have the opportunity to share a love of books and of literacy with all our students. We can provide our students with that comfortable relationship of older reader and younger reader sharing a favorite book. That memory of my high-school English teacher sitting on a desk reading aloud *King Lear* is forever etched in my mind as an example of how great a teacher's influence can be.

I have taught elementary school at all grade levels. What I have learned to appreciate is that the teaching of literacy — of reading and writing — is about empowerment. Matt Groening, best known as the creator and writer of *The Simpsons*, once said: "I can't believe it! Reading and writing actually paid off!" Your students need to discover this truth too.

I love reading and writing, and the sense of shared joy they offer. I love the written word. I love its power to inspire and uplift, and its ability to help us clarify our thoughts. I love reading the work of other authors: hearing their voices and relishing what they have to say. I love the act of writing: crafting sentences in just the right way. I love watching students empowered by the act of writing, too.

How to Begin

But I do understand that not all teachers feel this way about writing and teaching students how to do it. Perhaps you've suffered your way through this book well aware of your own neutral or negative feelings towards writing. Perhaps you find yourself having to teach writing to your students and you wonder where to begin ...

Begin by choosing your favorite picture book and deciding how it could be used as a mentor text for writing. Or, if that seems a bit daunting, begin by choosing the chapter in this book that spoke to you the most. Perhaps you want to attempt journal writing from a new perspective, or, you're curious about trying this seemingly too-good-to-be-true freewriting I have referred to time and time again. Don't feel as if you have to implement everything at once: choose one or two areas to focus on.

If you are reading this over your summer break, consider how you will structure your writing program differently for the next school year. What will change in your planning? How will you get your students writing more? How will you address any negative attitudes towards writing in your classroom? How will you inspire your students to love the written word?

Wherever you decide to begin, begin today!

Words really do change worlds.

Recommended Resources

For Teachers of Writing

Calkins, Lucy McCormick. *A Guide to the Writing Workshop.* Portsmouth, NH: Heinemann, 2006.

Culham, Ruth. *6 + 1 Traits of Writing: The Complete Guide for the Primary Grades.* New York: Scholastic, 2005.

———. *6 + 1 Traits of Writing: The Complete Guide Grades 3 and Up.* New York: Scholastic, 2003.

———. *The Writing Thief: Using Mentor Texts to Teach the Craft of Writing.* Portland, ME: Stenhouse, 2016.

Fletcher, Ralph. *Making Nonfiction from Scratch.* Portland, ME: Stenhouse, 2015.

Fox, Mem. *Radical Reflections: Passionate Opinions on Teaching, Learning, and Living.* San Diego, CA: Harcourt, 1993.

Gear, Adrienne. *Writing Power: Engaging Thinking through Writing.* Markham, ON: Pembroke, 2011.

Heard, Georgia, and Jennifer McDonough. *A Place for Wonder: Reading and Writing Nonfiction in the Primary Grades.* Portland, ME: Stenhouse, 2009.

Paley, Vivian Gussin. *The Girl with the Brown Crayon: How Children Use Stories to Shape Their Lives.* Cambridge, MA: Harvard University Press, 1997.

Rog, Lori. *Marvelous Minilessons for Teaching Nonfiction, Writing K–3.* Markham, ON: Pembroke, 2016.

Rog, Lori Jamison, and Donna-Lynn Galloway. *Reading, Writing, Playing, Learning.* Markham, ON: Pembroke, 2017.

Routman, Regie. *Read, Write, Lead: Breakthrough Strategies for Schoolwide Literacy Success.* Alexandria, VA: ASCD, 2014.

Shubitz, Stacey. *Craft Moves: Lesson Sets for Teaching Writing with Mentor Texts.* Portland, ME: Stenhouse, 2016.

For Aspiring Writers

Lamott, Anne. *Bird by Bird: Some Instructions on Writing and Life.* New York: Anchor Books, 1994.

Goldberg, Bonni. *Room to Write: Daily Invitations to a Writer's Life.* New York: Jeremy P. Tarcher/Putnam, 1996.

Goldberg, Natalie. *Writing Down the Bones: Freeing the Writer Within.* Boston: Shambhala Publications, 2005.

References

Atwell, Nancie. 2015. *In the Middle: A Lifetime of Learning about Writing, Reading and Adolescents*. 3rd ed. Portsmouth, NH: Heinemann.

Calkins, Lucy McCormick. 2006. *A Guide to the Writing Workshop*. Portsmouth, NH: Heinemann.

Calkins, Lucy, and Marjorie Martinelli. 2006. *Launching the Writing Workshop (Grades 3–5)*. Portsmouth, NH: Heinemann.

Cecil, Nancy Lee. 1994. *For the Love of Language: Poetry for Every Learner*. Winnipeg: Peguis.

Crowhurst, Marion. 1993. *Writing in the Middle Years*. Markham, ON: The Pippin Teacher's Library.

Culham, Ruth. 2003. *6+1 Traits of Writing: The Complete Guide Grades 3 and Up*. New York: Scholastic.

Elbow, Peter. 1994. "What Do We Mean When We Talk about Voice in Texts?" In *Voices on Voice: Perspectives, Definitions, Inquiry*, edited by K. Blake Yancey, 1–35. Urbana, IL: National Council of Teachers of English.

———. 1998. *Writing with Power: Techniques for Mastering the Writing Process*. 2nd ed. New York: Oxford University Press.

Fox, Mem. 1993. *Radical Reflections: Passionate Opinions on Teaching, Learning and Living*. New York: Harcourt Brace.

Gear, Adrienne. 2011. *Writing Power: Engaging Thinking through Writing*. Markham, ON: Pembroke.

Goldberg, Natalie. 1986. *Writing Down the Bones: Freeing the Writer Within*. Boston & London: Shambhala Publications.

Keene, Ellin Oliver, and Susan Zimmermann. 1997. *Mosaic of Thought*. Portsmouth, NH: Heinemann.

Laidlaw, Linda. 1998. "Finding 'Real' Lives: Writing and Identity." *Language Arts* 75 (2): 126–31.

Littky, Dennis, with Samantha Grabelle. 2004. *The Big Picture: Education Is Everyone's Business*. Alexandria, VA: ASCD.

McClay, Jill Kedersha, and Margaret Mackey. 2009. "Distributed Assessment in OurSpace: This Is Not a Rubric." In *Assessing New Literacies*, edited by Anne Burke and Roberta F. Hammett, 113–32. New York: Peter Lang.

Murray, Donald M. 2004. *The Craft of Revision*. 5th ed. Boston: Wadsworth.

Ontario Ministry of Education. 2006. *The Ontario Curriculum, Grades 1 to 8: Language*. Toronto: Ontario Ministry of Education.

Paley, Vivian Gussin. 1997. *The Girl with the Brown Crayon: How Children Use Stories to Shape Their Lives*. Cambridge, MA: Harvard University Press.

Robinson, Ken. 2009. *The Element: How Finding Your Passion Changes Everything*. New York: Penguin Books.

Rosen, Kim. 2009. *Saved by a Poem: The Transformative Power of Words*. New York: Hay House.

Routman, Regie. 2014. *Read, Write, Lead: Breakthrough Strategies for Schoolwide Literacy Success*. Alexandria, VA: ASCD.

Spandel, Vicki. 2001. *Creating Writers through 6-Trait Writing Assessment and Instruction*. 3rd ed. New York: Addison Wesley Longman.

Stead, Tony. 2002. *Is That a Fact? Teaching Nonfiction Writing K–3*. Portland, ME: Stenhouse.

Stockman, Angela. 2016. *Make Writing: 5 Teaching Strategies That Turn Writer's Workshop into a Maker Space*. Cleveland, OH: Times 10 Publications.

Trimble, John R. 1975. *Writing with Style: Conversations on the Art of Writing*. Englewood Cliffs, NJ: Prentice-Hall.

Index